HEART
OF THE
STORY
SERIES

THE
Family
of Jesus
BIBLE STUDY

KAREN
KINGSBURY

LifeWay Press®
Nashville, Tennessee

Published by LifeWay Press® ©2014 by Karen Kingsbury

The Family of Jesus ©2014 by Karen Kingsbury. Published by Howard Books; A Division of Simon & Schuster, Inc.; Brentwood, Tennessee 37027. Used by Permission

ISBN 978-1-4300-3489-6 • Item 005679769
Dewey decimal classification: 232.9

Subject headings FAMILY LIFE \ JESUS CHRIST—FAMILY AND FRIENDS\BIBLE—SOCIAL LIFE AND CUSTOMS

Unless otherwise noted all Scripture quotations are taken from the Holman Christian Standard Bible®, Copyright © 1999, 2000, 2002, 2003, 2009 by Holman Bible Publishers. Used by permission. Holman Christian Standard Bible®, Holman CSB®, and HCSB® are federally registered trademarks of Holman Bible Publishers. Scripture quotations marked AMP are taken from The Amplified® Bible, copyright © 1954, 1958, 1962, 1964, 1965, 1987 by The Lockman Foundation. Used by permission (*www.lockman. org*). Scripture marked NIV are taken from the Holy Bible, NEW INTERNATIONAL VERSION®. Copyright © 1973, 1978, 1984 by Biblica, Inc. All rights reserved worldwide. Used by permission. Scripture marked The Message is taken from The Message. Copyright © 1993, 1994, 1995, 1996, 2000, 2001, 2002. Used by permission of NavPress Publishing Group.

To order additional copies of this resource, write to LifeWay Church Resources Customer Service; One LifeWay Plaza; Nashville, TN 37234-0113; fax 615.251.5933; phone 800.458.2772; email *orderentry@lifeway.com;* order online at *www.lifeway.com;* or visit the LifeWay Christian Store serving you.

Printed in the United States of America

Adult Ministry Publishing, LifeWay Church Resources, One LifeWay Plaza, Nashville, TN 37234-0152

CONTENTS

ABOUT THE AUTHOR

Number-one *New York Times* best-selling author Karen Kingsbury is America's favorite inspirational novelist, with more than 20 million copies of her books in print. Her last dozen titles have reached the top of national lists.

Karen calls her work Life-Changing Fiction™ because of the response she hears from readers. She believes God puts a story on her heart, but He has a world full of other hearts in mind. "Only He could do that," Karen often says.

Karen and her husband, Don, and their six kids have Bibles all over the house and Scripture verses on the walls in every room. But no Bible will ever mean as much as the one Don still has, the one with the split down the binding that marked their confrontation before she became a Christian. It is proof that God takes what is broken and makes it beautiful again.

A popular speaker at women's groups around the country, Karen spends her spare time playing tennis and family games with her children, taking walks with Don, and being on-air for her national Salem/FISH afternoon radio program: "The Karen Kingsbury Show," airing weekdays, 2-7 p.m. Karen, with her daughter, Kelsey, also has a DaySpring card and gift line (Possibilities) in stores now. The line features favorite quotes from her books with Kelsey's designs.

Karen truly loves her reader friends, interacting daily with some 300,000 friends on Facebook and 50,000 followers on Twitter. But maybe what excites Karen most these days is her work on *The Family of Jesus Bible Study*.

"I wanted to use my storytelling to make people fall in love with the Bible," Karen says. "Family is important to me. So I started by taking a closer look at the family of Jesus. I was amazed at what I found." Karen believes the stories of these special, real-life people will impact your story in a very powerful way. They may even change your life.

TENTS AND STAKES

My goal with this Bible study was simple: Use my storytelling to help all of us fall in love with the Bible. But I knew that along the way I would need to mix Scripture and fiction to tell a more complete story of the characters in the family of Jesus.

So I began to look at this project as tent-building.

Scripture is very important to me. God's Holy Word is my absolute authority. For that reason, Bible verses on each of the family members of Jesus became my *tent stakes*. I anchored them deep into the ground and allowed nothing to move them.

Then I added a few more tent stakes—the historical and cultural absolutes of Jesus' day.

With those in place, it was time to paint the canvas. Tent material moves and billows between the tent stakes. Did Joseph bring wild orchids to Mary? Did he cry out to God for help on the way to Bethlehem? We don't know, but in my storytelling I believe he might have done so.

With the tent stakes of Scripture and cultural relevancy deeply embedded in the ground, I allowed myself to dream and imagine. Soon I began to write stories more beautiful than any God has given me.

The question for each story, each scene became this: *Was it possible?* If it was possible for the tent canvas to billow in the way of my storytelling, then I let it billow. In *The Family of Jesus Bible Study*, every time you see content that is screened and attributed to *The Family of Jesus* book, you can know that it is part of my imagining, storytelling, tent-billowing process.

The tent stakes of Scripture and biblical history in this Bible study will take you deeper into what we do know about each family member, into prophecies fulfilled, into Bible passages about character and obedience, and into each family member's unique role in God's redemption story through Jesus. Interactive questions, the group process, home study, and journaling all are a vital part of this study that can help you fall in love with Scripture.

Every story was approved by a pastor and the team at LifeWay for scriptural accuracy. Just to be sure the tent stakes were firmly in the ground.

What resulted were six stories that will make you feel deeply the cost and commitment for each of the family members of Jesus. Those stories can be found in my book *The Family of Jesus* (Howard Books, 2014).

My stories also resulted in this unbelievable Bible study—the one you are about to begin. The team at LifeWay filmed me in six unforgettable teaching and storytelling sessions before a life audience of women. In addition, I met with editorial experts at LifeWay to determine just the right Bible verses and questions to take you deeper into the family of Jesus.

I believe God will use this time to change your heart forever.

So … step into the tent and let the adventure begin.

ABOUT THIS STUDY

Elements of each session

YOUR STORY (START)—God desires to write His story on the hearts of His creation. Our stories are part of His story because He chooses to use us. So during this study I will be encouraging you to use wisely the days God has given you to write a well-crafted story with your life.

Be willing to share your experiences and insights with your group; they are important and will benefit other women. This opening time segment (approx. 15 min.) is when you get to know each other better. The bond that develops in your group will enrich your study and strengthen you spiritually.

THE BIBLE CHARACTER'S STORY; FOR EXAMPLE, JOSEPH'S STORY (WATCH, DISCUSS, and STUDY)—During session 1, for example, I teach about Joseph for about 30 minutes on video. Because I am a storyteller, I share the big picture of what Joseph's life might have been like and highlight several key principles from Scripture.

This time is the heart of the Bible study as, after the video, you interact with life-changing activities and questions prompted by the truth of Scripture. You will better see how each person in Jesus' family contributed to God's ongoing story of redemption and reconciliation. Each screened portion of content comes from *The Family of Jesus* book, giving your group a springboard for finding out more about this family member and for unpacking biblical truths and applications.

If possible, allow 45 to 60 minutes for the video and group interaction segment.

LIVING IN GOD'S STORY (GOING DEEPER)—This time of delving more into each Bible character happens between sessions. Use the additional readings as daily devotions, as an opportunity to search other Scriptures (especially Old Testament), and as markers of how God is working in your life and journey.

COMMITMENTS TO YOUR GROUP

Your experience with your group will be impacted by what you bring to it. Be willing to make personal commitments regarding preparation, confidentiality, respect, and accountability in order to have quality time together.

PREPARATION

To get the most out of each group session, try to read through the Watch, Discuss, and Study content each week and answer the questions so you are ready to discuss the material. You may also benefit from reading the hardback book *The Family of Jesus* (Howard Books) for Karen's collection of short stories on each Bible person.

CONFIDENTIALITY

You may be prompted to share thoughts, feelings, and experiences, and must be able to trust the group to keep personal information strictly confidential. Accept each other without judgment.

RESPECT

Respect each other's thoughts and opinions, providing a safe place for those insights to be shared without fear of judgment or unsolicited advice. If advice is requested, then lend your opinion, but season it with grace and offer it in love.

ACCOUNTABILITY

Commit to support and encourage each other during the sessions and to pray for each other between meetings. Setting up an email list can help women keep in touch.

JOSEPH: HUSBAND, PROTECTOR, SERVANT

Lots of men Joseph's age would have chosen Mary. But the friendship between Joseph and Mary's families worked in Joseph's favor and it became the answer to his prayers. It was really going to happen. He was going to marry the girl of his dreams.

"What are you thinking?" Mary's voice was soft, like music on the wind.

Joseph grinned. "How great God is, letting me have you for the rest of my life."

She looked down at her lap, her smile lifting her pretty mouth. . . . "I love talking to Him. Seeking His will." She found Joseph's eyes. "I've done that since I was a little girl."

Joseph took a deep breath and admired Mary. Everyone knew about her faith. More than any of the young women in town, Mary loved God, and the proof showed in her eyes.

THE FAMILY OF JESUS, *page 6*

Joseph, the earthly father of Jesus, is never quoted in Scripture, not even once. In fact, we have no record of anything ever spoken by him. The closest thing we see, in Matthew 1:21, is that he obediently named his son Jesus.

YOUR STORY

START

Everyone has a story. Your group is where you can share your story and hear from others, as together you learn about the family of Jesus.

Have you ever wondered what it would have been like to grow up in Jesus' home? What His siblings were like? What traditions the family observed? What made them laugh and cry?

> How would you describe your family to someone you have never met?

> Where did you live? How did your family make decisions? How did you feel about your brothers and sisters?

> If you were to create a family tree with three to six of the family members who have had the greatest impact on your life, who would you include and why?

For many of us, family is the setting in which we first learned about God.

> Can you recall a God-shaping event that led to your knowing Him or to experiencing some other good thing in your life?

God places us in families for good reasons (see Gen. 2:24; Ex. 20:12; Josh. 24:15; Ps. 103:17; 127:3-5). He has placed us in specific families for a reason, too.

When we first meet Joseph we're not sure how old he is, maybe late teens or early twenties. He is a carpenter in the family business in Nazareth. Nothing is out of the ordinary about Joseph except for one thing: he is a man who loves God.

> What would you most like to ask Joseph?

JOSEPH'S STORY

WATCH

Watch Joseph's story from The Family of Jesus Bible Study DVD *and discuss the questions with your group.*

We have to be very _____ with the Word of God and how we handle it.

Joseph knew he could never have any greater calling than to care for and protect Mary and Jesus, his Lord and Savior. What can we learn from the story of Joseph?

Matthew 1:19 (HCSB, "righteous"; NIV, "faithful to the law"; KJV, "just")

Joseph was a between-Sundays guy. He knew how to love and live, faithfully _____ to the _____ he was given.

May we all say, _____ _____. Let our house be a church.

When we really see Joseph, we can be _____ by what we learn; we can become more loyal, more trusting, more faithful, more aware of other people.

DISCUSS

As you listen to Joseph's story, what do you learn about his character?

How do you feel about God writing a story with the days of your life?

Video downloads of this session are available for purchase at *www.lifeway.com/karenkingsbury*

If you are on social media, share what you are learning *#familyofjesus*

STVDY

> *He ran his thumb along Mary's hand and breathed in deep, enjoying the clear spring air. "I feel like God has something big for us, Mary. Right here in Nazareth."*
>
> *"Like what?" She angled her head, admiration bright in her expression. "A bigger carpentry shop?"*
>
> *"Maybe." Joseph narrowed his eyes and watched the streaky sky. "I don't know. I just feel it." It was getting late so he helped her to her feet. "Whatever God has ahead, as long as I'm with you, I'm ready."*
>
> *Mary didn't say anything. The look in her eyes told him she agreed with every word and whatever God's plan for them, they were ready. They would face it together.*
>
> THE FAMILY OF JESUS, *pages 6-7*

A CHANGE OF PLANS

Read Matthew 1:18—20.

What plan was God revealing to these young adults?

Betrothed to the man she would marry, the young Mary, a virgin, learned from an angel that she was pregnant by the Holy Spirit. Mary was understandably frightened and confused about the angel's appearance and message.

Custom required couples to wait a year after a betrothal commitment to prepare for the solemn marriage relationship. Various translations of Matthew 1 describe Mary as "pledged" or "engaged," and verse 19 designates Joseph as "her husband." A betrothal contract was legally binding; only divorce or death could sever the vows.

If you had been in Mary's place, what would you fear telling Joseph?

If you had been in Joseph's shoes, what feelings do you think you would have had upon hearing Mary's news?

A DIFFICULT DECISION

Joseph didn't fly into a rage when he learned Mary was pregnant, as shocking as her news must have been. It was contrary to his nature. Questions likely bombarded him, though: *How could she have betrayed me and our dreams? She's talking about hearing from an angel; is she crazy as well as unfaithful?*

How do verses 19-20 describe a righteous response in an unheard-of situation?

This passage characterizes Joseph as "righteous," or right with God and in good standing with others. In this situation, Mary would be the object of ostracism and shame. According to the laws of the day, she could be stoned to death. Both families would be shunned. Joseph did not want to expose her to "public disgrace." *Father, please, protect my Mary …*

Not only did Joseph want to do the right thing, he wanted to do it in the right way. "But after he had considered these things" (v. 20) shows him working through a difficult decision, trying to process baffling circumstances and exercise patience before making a hard decision. *I trust You, God. But I never imagined this.*

As was his pattern, Joseph cried out to God and took the next step in faith, determined even in turmoil to find God's purpose for himself and for Mary.

What is the difference between reacting and responding?

Which do you do most?

TAKING THE NEXT STEP TOGETHER

Read Matthew 1:20–25.

What guidance did Joseph receive? From whom?

> *The Holy Spirit? Joseph felt the hair on his neck stand up. That's what Mary had said. Her words exactly. The baby in her was from God alone. He blinked a few times and nodded. "Mary told me that."*
>
> *A look of utter truth shone in the angel's face. "She will give birth to a son, and you are to give Him the name Jesus, because He will save His people from their sins."*
>
> THE FAMILY OF JESUS, *page 19*

Throughout the Bible, angels communicate significant actions or information to people. Through an angel, God reassured and directed Joseph when he needed it most. The angel confirmed to Joseph what had also been revealed to Mary.

What situation has most challenged your ability to trust?

How do you relate to Joseph?

This young man's trust in God would be challenged throughout his life. While Joseph allowed God to use him in His magnificent story of redemption, the ultimate story is God's.

LIVING IN GOD'S STORY

GOING DEEPER

Home study can help you better understand God's work in Joseph's life—and in your own. You may want to read the biblical narrative about Joseph, in Matthew 1:16–2:25 and Luke 1:26-38; 2:1-52. For more insights about Joseph in The Family of Jesus, *read chapter 1 (pp. 1-38).*

In learning to love Jesus more by studying the people who knew Him best, you can also discover principles for relating to your family. Use this unique opportunity to build a stronger home as you learn more about Jesus and His family.

DAY 1
WHEN THE TIME WAS RIGHT

Four hundred years of silence hung over the Jewish people since a prophet (Malachi) had spoken on behalf of God. Now all of Israel was waiting. For a sign or a prophet. For the Messiah.

The Hebrew word *Messiah* means "Anointed One"; *Christos*, or Christ, is its translation in Greek. Jesus, the name Joseph was to give the Son born of the Holy Spirit (Matt. 1:20-21), means "Yahweh saves" or "the Lord saves."[1] Salvation of sins would be for "His people." The fact that only God can save—we cannot save ourselves—is even expressed in identifying the Son of God.

In the New Testament, Matthew, Mark, Luke, and John uniquely share the good news of Jesus as the Promised One. Matthew shows how the Messiah is the fulfillment of Old Testament prophecies, especially resonating with his Jewish audience. Luke, a Gentile and early church historian, highlights Jesus as fully divine Son of God and fully human Son of Man, identifying with all our needs and sorrows.

Read each prophecy and corresponding Old Testament Scripture (left column). Draw lines to match the prophecy to its New Testament fulfillment (right column). How do you see God preparing the world for the Messiah?

OLD TESTAMENT PROPHECY	NEW TESTAMENT FULFILLMENT
Jesus would be:	
Born of a woman (Genesis 3:15)	Matthew 1:22-23; Luke 1:26-31
Born in Bethlehem (Micah 5:2)	Matthew 2:1; Luke 2:4-6
Born of a virgin (Isaiah 7:14)	Luke 1:32-33; Romans 1:3
Descended from Abraham (Genesis 12:3; 22:18)	Matthew 1:20; Galatians 4:4
Heir to King David's throne (2 Samuel 7:12-13; Isaiah 9:7)	Matthew 1:1; Romans 9:5; Galatians 3:8,16

While the people had not heard from God for so long, He was at work creating the perfect time for His Son to come to earth. Many things were working together for the one who would prepare the way for the Messiah, for Jesus' ministry, and for the writing of the New Testament.

History tells us there were six major Israelite time periods immediately before and including the 400 years of silence: Persian, highlighted by Cyrus' overcoming the Babylonian Empire and the Temple being rebuilt; Greek, with Alexander the Great; Egyptian, with Ptolemy; Syrian, with Antiochus III the Great and Antiochus IV Epiphanes; Maccabean, with Judas Maccabeus; and Roman, which included Herod and Caesar. (Also see the article "What Happened During Those 400 Years?", p. 140.)

The Romans built vast road systems that made it easier for the early Christians to spread the gospel. Also, the Greek language spread throughout the world, making it easier for people to communicate.

Exodus 32 describes how, centuries earlier, the Israelites rebelled when Moses stayed on the mountain for 40 days. Now God had been silent 400 years!

In what sense do you think God's people had made progress in faithfulness? In what sense do you think they were practicing the same old unfaithfulness?

Think of our society today. In what ways have we made progress in waiting for God to speak and in obeying Him? How have we stayed the same or even gotten worse?

Now think about your life. How have you grown in godliness? In what ways do you struggle with the same old temptations or sins?

In Old Testament times, a divinely-appointed task was often connected to an office such as prophet or king. These leaders were viewed as anointed or designated for a special task by Yahweh, Israel's God. Israelite kings, beginning with Saul and especially referring to David, were particularly viewed as Yahweh's anointed. The oracle spoken by Nathan in 2 Samuel 7:12-16 reflects the hope of Israel for David's dynasty to continue for succeeding generations and to include the Messiah.[2] The Jews linked the inauguration of God's new kingdom to the kingdom of Israel, which would never end.

Focused on the hope of a Messiah from King David's lineage, Joseph's generation was pinning their hopes on a royal Messiah, a powerful king. They anticipated triumphant, resounding victory over their oppressors—not the quiet whisper of an infant's cry.

Read Luke 2:1–18.

> *I believe you, Father. I do. But sometimes I wonder if I've missed something along the way. He [Joseph] glanced at the manger. A feeding trough? For the King of the world? Bugs and animals and flies? Joseph wasn't sure what he had expected for the child's birth, but he hadn't expected this.*
>
> THE FAMILY OF JESUS, *page 28*

What expectations do you have of the Son of God?

Compare the angels' declaration of Jesus' birth, in Luke 2, to Paul's description of Jesus' nature, in Philippians 2:

> But the angel said to them, "Don't be afraid, for look, I proclaim to you good news of great joy that will be for all the people: Today a Savior, who is Messiah the Lord, was born for you in the city of David. This will be the sign for you: You will find a baby wrapped snugly in cloth and lying in a feeding trough." Suddenly there was a multitude of the heavenly host with the angel, praising God and saying: Glory to God in the highest heaven, and peace on earth to people He favors!
> LUKE 2:10-14

> Make your own attitude that of Christ Jesus, who, existing in the form of God, did not consider equality with God as something to be used for His own advantage.

> Instead He emptied Himself by assuming the form of a slave, taking on the likeness of men.

> And when He had come as a man in His external form, He humbled Himself by becoming obedient to the point of death—even to death on a cross.

> For this reason God highly exalted Him and gave Him the name that is above every name, so that at the name of Jesus every knee will bow—of those who are in heaven and on earth and under the earth—and every tongue should confess that Jesus Christ is Lord, to the glory of God the Father.
> PHILIPPIANS 2:5-11

For Jesus to come to earth as a helpless baby rather than a powerful ruler was the epitome of humility. God's Son willingly gave up His rights and His throne, becoming flesh to live among us, revealing the Father to us (see John 1:14), Jesus fully identified with humanity, yet was without sin. In Him, we see both the love and power of God.

Be assured that one day He *will* return as King of kings and Lord of lords, and every knee will bow and every tongue will confess that Jesus Christ is Lord (see Rom. 14:11).

Read Galatians 4:4–5.

> When the time came to completion, God sent His Son, born of a woman, born under the law, to redeem those under the law, so that we might receive adoption as sons.

What relationship did Jesus come to establish?

How do you praise God for the gift of His Son?

ACTS ONLY GOD CAN EXPLAIN

God continued to reveal His direction and plan for Joseph and His new family. From protecting them to reaffirming Jesus' identity and purpose, God used Joseph and found him faithful.

Humble shepherds witnessed the glory of His birth announcement to the world— and went to worship Him. The Holy Spirit prompted Elizabeth, Mary's cousin who was pregnant with the forerunner of Jesus, to affirm the significance of both Jesus and John in God's kingdom (see Luke 1:39-45).

As Jesus grew, those who would harm Jesus had begun to look for Him. As God directed, again through an angel, Joseph protected the woman he loved and the Christ child entrusted to them by taking them to Egypt and back to Nazareth when it was safe. Searching until they found Him, wise men came to worship Him and went home a different way, avoiding Herod (see Matt. 2).

The very nature of providential acts of God is that they often are subtle or hidden.

> Identify a difficult or painful episode that seemed entirely bad at the time, but has born good fruit in your life.

Read Luke 2:36–38.

> *The woman was old like Simeon, and like Simeon, she knew Jesus. Despite the crowd, and all the chaos and confusion, she knew Him.*
>
> *She touched the child's head and smiled into Mary and Joseph's eyes. "This is the Savior of the world," she whispered. "Thanks be to God for saving His people!" And then with all the happiness of the greatest celebration ever, Anna turned to the crowd around them and shouted with joy. "This is the Savior of the world! Thanks be to God! Thanks to our great and mighty Father!"*
>
> *The happy moment was another sign from God, reassuring Joseph that all was well and that the Lord was with them. Both the baby in their keeping, and the Father above.*
>
> THE FAMILY OF JESUS, *page 33*

How do you explain the "coincidences" of your life?

What do you attribute only to God?

Simeon and Anna may have been the first to publicly recognize the young child as the long-awaited Messiah. Still faithful, both had grown old as they patiently waited for the Promised One, and God graced these humble servants with the privilege of seeing the Messiah in their lifetime.

In keeping with the Law of Moses regarding the firstborn son, Mary and Joseph took Jesus to the temple to be consecrated; scholars estimate Jesus was six weeks old. Once there, the family was approached by Simeon, who had been told by the Holy Spirit that he would not die until he saw the Messiah (see Luke 2:26).

Simeon, like Joseph, was "righteous and devout" (Luke 2:25). The same Holy Spirit led Simeon to the temple that day:

> Guided by the Spirit, he entered the temple complex. When the parents brought in the child Jesus to perform for Him what was customary under the law, Simeon took Him up in his arms, praised God, and said: "Now, Master, You can dismiss Your slave in peace, as You promised. For my eyes have seen Your salvation. You have prepared it in the presence of all peoples—a light for revelation to the Gentiles and glory to Your people Israel." His father and mother were amazed at what was being said about Him.
> LUKE 2:27-33

Such moments were clear signs from God, reassuring Joseph that the Lord was with them still. What had happened—and was still to come—only God could fully explain.

PROTECTED AND PROTECTOR

> *Angry, desperate, heartbroken tears. No matter what Mary had done, regardless of*
> *the reason, he still loved her. He couldn't bear to see her stoned to death. They might*
> *as well stone him, too. The sobs shook his shoulders and made it hard to breathe. What*
> *was he supposed to do? He wiped his face with the back of his hands and stood, looking*
> *one direction and then the next. As if there might be some way out. But there was none.*
> *None except one.*
>
> THE FAMILY OF JESUS, *pages 16-17*

Betrayal. Is there anything worse than feeling that someone you trust failed you and broke a confidence or promise? It is more than disappointment or head knowledge of the failure. Betrayal produces a moral and psychological conflict that goes to the heart and is deeply rooted in emotion. Joseph faced what appeared to be betrayal by Mary. Think about all that Joseph must have experienced when he found out she was pregnant (before the angel revealed the truth to him).

> *Joseph lifted his eyes to the hills, his jaws clenched. "Where does my help come from?"*
> *The broken cry filled the air. He pushed on, determined. "My help comes from the Lord."*
> *He gritted his teeth even as hot tears made their way down his cheek. "The Maker of*
> *heaven and earth."*
>
> *Yes, the psalmist was right. Joseph had known the words to the Holy Scriptures since he*
> *was a boy. They had never meant more. "Help me, God . . . You neither slumber nor sleep.*
> *Help me now."*
>
> THE FAMILY OF JESUS, *page 17*

Read Psalm 121.

How might the psalmist's words have comforted Joseph and given him courage to face the future?

Which words or phrases from Psalm 121 fly off the page to give you hope?

When there is such trust in God, there is an accompanying patience and peace that is hard to understand or explain. Philippians 4:4-7 comes close to describing this phenomenon, but until you see it lived out in your life, such peace often seems unattainable. Knowing that the Lord is your Protector, you can walk through the most challenging situations and circumstances.

What does it feel like to be protected? What does it feel like to be responsible for someone else's safety and protection?

In what situation right now do you need God to show Himself as your Protector? How will you cling to the truths of Psalm 121 as you face this situation and develop patient trust?

Pray that God will show you in a way you can recognize, that He is your Protector. Know that you can trust Him even when He appears to be silent.

EXPECTANT IN WAITING, JOYFUL IN HOPE

> *"My name is Simeon," he told Joseph. "Please, may I hold the child?"*
>
> *Joseph sensed he had nothing to fear from Simeon. He carefully handed Jesus over. What happened next would stay with Joseph and Mary forever. With Jesus in his arms, the old man stared up at the sky and proclaimed that he could die in peace now because his eyes had seen the salvation come for all people.*
>
> THE FAMILY OF JESUS, *page 32*

Read Luke 2:25—38.

So after all their watching and waiting, how did Simeon and Anna know Him? What significant signs and wonders occurred when Mary and Joseph brought Jesus into the temple?

Simeon and Anna had no need for signs, wonders, or great displays of fireworks. Why? They knew Jesus because they both spent time with God in prayer, searching the Scriptures and waiting patiently for God to reveal His Son, our Savior. They were in tune with God's Spirit. They could see, hear, and sense God because they spent time with Him and waited patiently for Him to reveal the One for whom they were looking.

To what extent do you spend time with God as you wait patiently for Him to reveal truth, answers, direction, guidance, and counsel?

How would you describe your thoughts and emotions when you find yourself in a waiting period and all you hear is silence?

Search these verses from Scripture for what they tell you about waiting on the Lord: Psalm 37:7; Psalm 40:1-5; Psalm 62:5-8; Psalm 86:15; and Isaiah 40:28-31. Describe your thoughts.

What do these verses tell you about the nature of God?

How does His character reassure you when you are in waiting mode?

As we trust God, resting in His presence and peace, we can experience, like Simeon and Anna, the amazing power of seeing God work. He may work in ways that other people miss—and we see because we are waiting for Him to appear and work.

Often it is in the whispers that we hear God most clearly. Sometimes, when you spend time with Him daily seeking truth from His Word, He is so close you can almost feel His breath against your ear, whispering truth to you.

Commit to spend time in prayer, asking God to help you recognize how close He truly is. Look for His words of encouragement in the Bible as you wait patiently for the next steps and the answers He has for you.

ABOUT HIS FATHER'S WORK

Read Luke 2:39–52.

As Jesus grew, both His Heavenly Father and earthly father were pouring into Him. Joseph was watching his oldest boy grow and mature. Yet, there still was so much he would never fully understand.

Every year Jesus' family went to Jerusalem for the Passover festival. When He was 12 years old, Jesus joined them.

According to Luke 2:42-44, what happened on the way home?

Frantic, after three days of looking for Jesus, His parents found Him in the temple complex, listening and asking questions of the rabbis. "And all those who heard Him were astounded at His understanding and His answers" (Luke 2:47).

When Mary and Joseph found Jesus and asked Him about His absence, He explained, "Didn't you know that I had to be in My Father's house?" (Luke 2:49).

> *Though Jesus returned with them to Nazareth, and though He remained obedient, His words stayed with Joseph. Never mind the rescue from Bethlehem or Egypt. It didn't matter what Joseph had done to protect Jesus or how much he loved Mary. Forget the reality that Joseph had been there from the beginning. Joseph would never be Jesus's father.*
>
> *That role belonged to God alone.*
>
> THE FAMILY OF JESUS, *page 35*

Joseph's questioning, insights into his own purpose as well as Jesus' role, and reflections were part of a process that began before Jesus was born. Both earthly parents treasured in their hearts all God had revealed to them about their Son and His destiny.

Can you think of something you would have missed out on had you not stopped to consider an alternative? Explain.

How did this unexpected change turn into a new way for God to use you?

How might families today view their children as belonging to God?

Joseph did what he could, raising the Savior, loving His mother, picking wild orchids for Mary when she needed a reason to smile. Some seasons and years he felt too small for the task. Not brave enough or wise enough or strong enough. But then Joseph would remember the journey to Bethlehem or the one to Egypt. The times when Jesus was too small and Mary too weak. God had chosen him to protect the Savior and His mother back then, and Joseph would continue to do so as long as the Lord allowed.

THE FAMILY OF JESUS, *page 36*

According to Luke 3:23, Jesus "was thought to be the son of Joseph." We have no indication that Joseph ever relinquished any of his responsibility as Jesus' earthly father or bragged about who his Son really was. From what we know from Scripture, Joseph was content to serve God quietly and faithfully by being a great dad, servant, protector, and friend.

How does your service to God and your family enable you to be a faithful servant, protector, and friend?

She looked long into Joseph's eyes. "Thank you. For hearing God's voice. For rescuing us."

Joseph took her hands. He had never loved her more. "You are my life, Mary. You and Jesus. The promise I made to you will remain my purpose as long as I live. But the rescue comes from God alone. Always from Him."

THE FAMILY OF JESUS, *page 31*

ZECHARIAH: SINGING A NEW SONG

> *In those early days, Zechariah could see the future as easily as the sunrise. They would have a house full of children, girls like Elizabeth and sons to carry on the line of priestly duties.*
>
> *There would be laughter and long walks, the joy of happy children in their home, and a purpose of raising the next generation for God.*
>
> *But life hadn't played out that way.*
>
> THE FAMILY OF JESUS, *page 41*

Zechariah lived out his story against the tapestry of a life going in unexpected directions, with unfulfilled expectations. His is a story of preparing his heart for a son, and wondering when and how and why.
A story of singing and praise, after months of silence.

Precious John, prayed for so long, had finally come, not only to Zechariah's family but to the entire world, as forerunner for the Savior. "Praise the Lord, the God of Israel, because He has visited and provided redemption for His people" (Luke 1:68).

YOUR STORY

START

Everyone has a story. Enjoy sharing yours and hearing from your group as together you learn about another person in the family of Jesus—Zechariah.

Last week during home study you examined how some Old Testament prophecies were fulfilled in Jesus. You considered how coincidences of your life were part of God's timing. You witnessed how Mary and Joseph encountered two faithful servants of God, who recognized Jesus as the promised Messiah.

Discuss answers to these questions from day 3:

> What does it feel like to be protected? What does it feel like to be responsible for someone else's safety and protection?

As you begin to learn about Zechariah, look for ways his family intersected Jesus' family. Think about:

> How did you celebrate the birth of your first child or of a niece or nephew?

> What is the significance of your name?

ZECHARIAH'S STORY

WATCH

Watch Zechariah's story from The Family of Jesus Bible Study DVD *and discuss the questions with your group.*

Jesus' uncle prayed for the child he had longed for all his married life and for Elizabeth to no longer feel shame. What can we learn from Zechariah's story?

So many times, something happens in life that is not what we expected. Like Zechariah, we are called to be _____.

Luke 1:6-7

Luke 1:62-63

God wants us to believe _____ what we can see and hear.

John 16:33

God gives _____ to us in our story. He is why we can trust in the midst of trouble.

DISCUSS

Have you ever had trouble believing something was different from what your eyes saw or your ears heard? Share an example with the group.

How do you demonstrate trust when you are living according to God's guidelines and things still don't turn out as you expect?

Video downloads of this session are available for purchase at *www.lifeway.com/karenkingsbury*

If you are on social media, share what you are learning *#familyofjesus*

STUDY
WAITING AND WATCHING

Zechariah's fervent desires were twofold: for Elizabeth to bear a son and to see the Messiah. He and Elizabeth had prayed seemingly forever for a child. Both very old, these servants continued to pray in faith, despite the apparent impossibility humanly.

Centuries earlier, King David had divided the priesthood into 24 divisions, with each serving at the sanctuary for one week every six months (see 1 Chron. 24:5-10). Their tradition of service continued. Zechariah, "a priest of Abijah's division," was also "chosen by lot" … to "enter the sanctuary of the Lord and burn incense" (Luke 1:5,9). This was a sacred responsibility.

His wife, Elizabeth, was from Aaron's line. Any children born to these two would carry on important priestly roles.

Read Luke 1:5–6.

How were Zechariah and Elizabeth described in Luke 1:6? Does this description remind you of someone else in Jesus' family?

Compare the angel's announcement to Zechariah (Luke 1:13-17) with Gabriel's proclamation to Mary (Luke 1:30-37). Note similarities and differences.

SIMILARITIES   DIFFERENCES

How did Zechariah and Mary respond in a similar way (see vv. 18,34)?

Read Isaiah 40:3–5.

What prophecy is indicated by these Old Testament verses?

Read Luke 1:13–17 and 3:2–6.

Who fulfilled this forerunner role?

> *What? … This news from the angel was more than he [Zechariah] could take. Had he heard correctly? His son was going to prepare the way for the Lord? He had always believed, always prayed. Even when others would've long given up, Zechariah held out hope. But the idea that his son might be a modern-day Elijah?*
>
> THE FAMILY OF JESUS, *page 48*

Not only would Zechariah and Elizabeth have a miracle child after all these years, but he would play a special role in God's kingdom.

What question did Zechariah ask Gabriel, in Luke 1:18?

The angel answered Zechariah's "How can I know this?" by identifying himself and his purpose—and the authority behind his presence. Gabriel, "who stands in the presence of God," was sent specifically to tell Zechariah this good news (Luke 1:19.)

Yet, because he did not believe, Zechariah would remain silent and unable to speak until the events of Luke 1:13-17 were "fulfilled in their proper time" (v. 20).

The priest's question and concerns seem logical from a human perspective. As righteous and godly as Zechariah was, he still was learning about faith. He was reminded that God is faithful to fulfill His promises, but that He often does so in ways far beyond the ordinary. During his time of silence, Zechariah would discover more about God's working to prepare for both John and Jesus' coming.

How do silence and solitude help you focus on God?

The miracle God was doing didn't involve only their unborn son, John, it involved Mary and her unborn baby, too. More than that, Mary was carrying the Lord. The Savior of the world. Zechariah looked around. It was as if they were all standing on holy ground.

Elizabeth looked at Mary again, and this time tears brimmed in her eyes. She repeated the words she'd said earlier, this time in a whisper. "But why am I so favored, that the mother of my Lord should come to me?"

"The angel Gabriel told me about your baby. He said that nothing was impossible with God. I thought you might help me know how to do this. If I stayed a while."

THE FAMILY OF JESUS, *page 54*

In what ways do you need to internalize right now the truth that "nothing will be impossible with God" (Luke 1:37)?

How does "staying a while" with a trusted friend help you determine the direction to take? "Staying a while" with the Lord?

SINGING A NEW SONG

There was no reason to name the infant John other than it was God's command. Once Zechariah insisted that the child's name was John, he could speak again—and sing!

Record specific ways Zechariah praised God in Luke 1:67-79.

> Then his father Zechariah was filled with the Holy Spirit and prophesied: Praise the Lord, the God of Israel, because He has visited and provided redemption for His people.
>
> He has raised up a horn of salvation for us in the house of His servant David, just as He spoke by the mouth of His holy prophets in ancient times; salvation from our enemies and from the clutches of those who hate us.
>
> He has dealt mercifully with our fathers and remembered His holy covenant— the oath that He swore to our father Abraham. He has given us the privilege, since we have been rescued from our enemies' clutches, to serve Him without fear in holiness and righteousness in His presence all our days.
>
> And child, you will be called a prophet of the Most High, for you will go before the Lord to prepare His ways, to give His people knowledge of salvation through the forgiveness of their sins.
>
> Because of our God's merciful compassion, the Dawn from on high will visit us to shine on those who live in darkness and the shadow of death, to guide our feet into the way of peace.

Journal some ways you would like to praise God.

LIVING IN GOD'S STORY

GOING DEEPER

Home study can help you better understand God's work in Zechariah's life—and in your own. You may want to read the biblical narrative about Zechariah, in Matthew 2 and Luke 1. For more insights about Zechariah in The Family of Jesus, *read chapter 2 (pp. 39-67).*

In learning to love Jesus more by studying the people who knew Him best, you can also discover principles for relating to your family. Use this unique opportunity to build a stronger home as you learn more about Jesus and His family.

DAY 1

GOD'S FAITHFULNESS THROUGH GENERATIONS

In all parts of the world, in all cultures, people sing.

What are physical, mental, emotional, and spiritual benefits of singing? How do you think and feel when you catch yourself singing?

Physically

Mentally

Emotionally

Spiritually

Often when we sing, something happens to take our eyes off our concerns and circumstances. Singing brings people together. It unites those who are divided by opinions, race, religion, and other differences.

Zechariah was representing Israel as he sang. After months of silence, he praises and he sings. Spiritually, he was demonstrating that the one thing that was blocking Israel from God—their need for a Savior—was being removed. They too could sing again.

> How does Zechariah's song show God's unfolding plan from Old Testament days to the coming of the Messiah? Look up Matthew 1:67-79 in your Bible or use page 39 to view this song of praise.

Luke 1:69-70	The Messiah would be heir to King David's throne, establishing a lasting kingdom. *Read 2 Samuel 7:12-13; Isaiah 9:7; Luke 7:16; Hebrews 1:8-9.*
Luke 1:70-75	As early as His covenant with Abraham, God had promised a Rescuer and Redeemer. *Read Genesis 22:16-18; Psalm 105:8-10; Hosea 1:10; Acts 3:24-26.*
Luke 1:76-77	John's role of preparing the way of the Lord, much like that of a prophet, was important to the Messiah's ministry. *Read Isaiah 40:3; Malachi 3:1; Hebrews 6:20.*

From Abraham to kings to prophets, God's plan from the beginning included redemption and rescue, forgiveness and salvation. Zechariah, Elizabeth, and John were privileged to be a part of the final stages of His incarnation and revelation.

> *He [Zechariah] spent as many hours as he could holding John and rocking him, staring into his face and wondering about the things this child would do in years to come. How would he prepare the way for the Lord? What would that look like? The future would certainly be very bright indeed—especially for their John.*
>
> *Zechariah could only thank God that he and Elizabeth were chosen to be the boy's parents. Surely goodness and mercy would follow all of them for the rest of their days. Nobody's future looked as bright as theirs.*
>
> THE FAMILY OF JESUS, *page 58*

ASK, WAIT, PRAISE

God wants you to ask Him for a spouse. For a job. For financial relief. For rescue from temptation. For a heavy need on your heart.

Read Matthew 7:7–12.

Why do you think God enjoys being asked?

What keeps you from asking more from Him?

> *Zechariah was nothing if not faithful. As long as God gave him the ability to pray, he would ask for a miracle.*
>
> THE FAMILY OF JESUS, *page 40*

Zechariah and Elizabeth were ordinary people living ordinary lives, but with some painful, unfilled expectations. From our perspective of fast-paced lives and immediate gratification, they seemed to be in long-term waiting mode.

While Zechariah and Elizabeth waited, they prayed—and watched and listened for how God would answer. Prayer is how we, too, present our requests to Him, even as our Heavenly Father already knows our needs.

Recall a time when God's answer to a prayer met the need of your heart in a much better way than you had hoped.

In your waiting, enjoy and engage in the asking, even when prayer seems repetitive. And when God's answer comes, praise Him, even when the answer is different from what you wanted.

The Father enjoys your praise, just as He enjoys your asking in faith (see Zeph. 3:17). Know that of all the gifts you will ever ask for or need, He has already given the best answer: redemption. In Zechariah's words, "Praise be to the Lord!" (Luke 1:68, NIV).

Zechariah had a song in his heart, a song that had built during his months of silence. The first thing he did when he could speak again was sing praises to God.

How can you cultivate a song of joy that overflows and sustains you?

Try writing a praise to God using special events from your own spiritual journey. You can use Zechariah's song (Luke 1:67-79; p. 39) as an example.

WHEN PRAYERS SEEM TO GO UNANSWERED

If we are honest, there are times when we feel as if our prayers make it to the ceiling and go no farther. We wonder if God hears us. Is He too busy? Does He not care about this situation or circumstance?

Have you been praying for something for a long time? Does it seem like God has not heard your prayers or does not wish to answer them?

Write a few of those prayers or the name of the person or need for which you have been praying.

How do you think Zechariah and Elizabeth felt after years of praying and waiting for a child of their own? You know they had to wonder why God had not answered their prayers for a child.

Record what you imagine were some of their thoughts and feelings as their prayers for a child went unanswered.

Read Luke 1:5—7.

Zechariah and Elizabeth were faithful to God. They served and obeyed Him. And yet, their prayer for a child continued to go unanswered. Even the most faithful and godly people experience unanswered prayers. They may experience confusion and long trials. Zechariah and Elizabeth should remind us that we should keep praying as long as the desire is there. What seemed like too long or too late ended up far exceeding their hopes. And the answer came at just the right time, God's timing!

Read Luke 18:1 and 1 Thessalonians 5:17.

Sometimes, what seems a hopeless situation or denial from God is only a delay.

How do these verses encourage you as you pray about a desire on your heart or a need that seems unmet?

What do you need to continue praying about?

However, at times, God does not change our circumstances. Instead of changing our situation and answering our prayers the way we wish, He changes us. He may gradually lessen the desire and change our hearts and our prayers to line up with His ultimate plan and purposes.

God could have prepared the way for the coming Savior any number of ways. Zechariah and Elizabeth could have given birth to John earlier in life. An angel might not have pronounced John's birth. Zechariah might not have experienced long years of unanswered prayers and the pregnancy of Elizabeth without a voice. But isn't the way God did it so much more miraculous, and so clearly His work!

The way God works often is miraculous and cannot be explained. It is during those times that no one else is able to take credit or justify how something happened other than to know that God was in it.

When have you experienced the miraculous works and wonders of God?

How will you continue to have hope when it seems your prayers go unanswered?

DAY 4

A SET-APART CHILD

Read Luke 1:17–19 and Malachi 4:6.

Zechariah's son, John, would have a very specific purpose. He and Elizabeth must not only train up his child, but rear him in such a way that John understood how God had set him apart. There was a design on his life. Things were about to change. Redemption was at hand!

> How is bringing up the next generation to know God part of your intentional parenting? Be ready to share ideas with other parents in your group.

Read Luke 1:13–14.

Every day Zechariah thanked God for the joy John brought to their home, and the delight he was in their lives. Zechariah and John often held long conversations out back, studying the sky and stars and handiwork of God's creation ...

Each year, the night before John's birthday, Zechariah and Elizabeth would wait until John was asleep. Then they'd quietly step into his room and pray over him—holding on to the boy he'd been at five or six or seven years old ... as long as they could. Some moments Zechariah wanted only to stop the sun from setting—so they could enjoy John a little longer.

THE FAMILY OF JESUS, *page 62*

John was a "joy and delight" (v. 14) to his parents and, because of his purpose, many had rejoiced at his birth.

What are some ways parents today commit their children to the Lord?

Parents turn the hearts of children toward God in meaningful ways: a nightly blessing or prayer; a baby dedication, committing the child to God and asking the church to help him or her learn about God; teaching children to pray and letting them hear you pray; talking with them about God; showing them God by their example.

You may have some other ideas. Share them here.

How are you preparing your children to leave your care and follow God's plan, using the foundation of faith already laid?

To his infant son, Zechariah exclaimed: "And child, you will be called a prophet of the Most High, for you will go before the Lord to prepare His ways, to give His people knowledge of salvation through the forgiveness of their sins" (Luke 1:76-77).

At the same time Zechariah and Elizabeth received John gratefully, they prepared to release him back to God.

NAMES HAVE MEANING

Zechariah thought back to those days when he couldn't speak. "God used the days of silence. He put a song in my heart but I couldn't sing it until the right time." Zechariah smiled at his boy. "The right time was the moment we named you John. Then I could speak, and the first thing I did was praise God with the song.

THE FAMILY OF JESUS, *pages 65-66*

"Do not fear, for I have redeemed you; I have called you by your name; you are Mine."
ISAIAH 43:1

What have your parents told you about the background behind your name?

How does their thought about your name make you feel special?

Names are important.

Your name is how you are identified. It captures a lot about your personality. Most of us like to be called by name, and sometimes are even offended if someone calls us by the wrong name. Your parents likely had a reason for giving you your name; it's part of your heritage and story. Your name is significant.

Names hold importance in Scripture, too. God instructed Zechariah to name his son John when there was no apparent reason to do so. Zechariah's name means "The Lord has remembered" and Elizabeth's name means "My God has sworn an oath."

Considering their stories, what significance do you find in these meanings of the names Zechariah and Elizabeth?

Similar naming took place elsewhere in Scripture.

Read Isaiah 7:14; Matthew 1:20–23; and Luke 1:31–32.

What names referring to Jesus do you discover?

According to Tony Evans, in *The Power of God's Names,* there is significance in names that goes back for centuries:

> Jesus is the New Testament equivalent of the Old Testament name Joshua, which means *salvation.* Joshua and Jesus. The two names create an interesting link, given that Joshua was a primary agent in rescuing God's chosen people from slavery in Egypt and delivering them to the promised land.[3]

Read Joshua 1:1–9.

What similarities do you see between Joshua and Jesus in these verses?

What differences do you see?

Evans continues:

> The other Old Testament character who bears a strong link with Immanuel is David, a former shepherd who rose to become the king of Israel and was described as a man after God's own heart (see 1 Sam. 13:14).[4]

Read 2 Samuel 7:12–13. Compare with Luke 1:32–33.

How do these verses point to Jesus?

Evans continues:

> It's important for us to remember that God established the promise of Immanuel—the promise of God with Us—thousands of years before Jesus arrived on earth. Long before Mary, the shepherds, and the wise men, God had planned to reveal Himself in a new way to His people. He'd planned to reveal Himself as Savior and rescue us from our sins. He'd planned to establish a new kingdom forever so that we could always know and experience Immanuel—God with Us.[5]

What does knowing God forever as *Immanuel*—God with us—mean to you? Take a moment to thank Him for His constant presence in your life.

Exploring more about the names of God can take your personal worship and Bible study to a new level. Learn how to worship in true humility as you better understand your humanity in light of God's deity, omniscience, and power. Calling on His name can impact how you pray and obey Him.

Two resources that unpack the names of God are *The Power of God's Names* by Tony Evans and *Knowing God by Name* by Mary A. Kassian. Enjoy your study!

JOHN THE BAPTIST: COMPLETING GOD'S TASK

The people were amazed, and many lined up to be baptized in the Jordan River. A few days passed, and still more people came. Among them were tax collectors looking to be baptized. As they drew near to the water, they called out, "Teacher, what should we do?"

John felt compassion toward them, but he knew their sins because God had shown him. "Don't collect any more than you are required to."

Soldiers came next. "And what should we do?"

Again John knew their hearts. "Don't force people to give you money. Don't bring false charges against people." He looked straight through them, to their hearts. "Be happy with your pay."

The crowds grew larger. After hundreds of years of silence, they wondered if John might be the Christ.

THE FAMILY OF JESUS, *pages 77-78*

"His name is John." His coming is an answer to prayer in so many ways.

"Teacher, what should we do?" John has words of repentance to hear and obey.

"Repent, and be baptized." John felt compassion for the people.

YOUR STORY

START

Everyone has a story. Enjoy sharing yours and hearing from your group as together you learn about another person in Jesus' family—John the Baptist.

Share how you answered some questions from last week's home study:

> Why do you think God enjoys hearing us ask Him to meet our needs when He already knows what those needs are? (day 2)

> Share a time you experienced a miraculous work or wonder of God. (day 3)

As we begin to learn more about John the Baptist, talk together about:

> Has it been a new idea for you to think about Bible people having dreams, friendships, vocations, and families? Experiencing pain, fear, and joy? How is this perspective bringing Scripture alive for you?

> Share a favorite opening act for a concert or other special occasion. How did it create energy and anticipation for the main event?

JOHN THE BAPTIST'S STORY

WATCH

Watch John the Baptist's story from The Family of Jesus Bible Study DVD *and discuss the questions with your group.*

John's greatest desire was to serve the Lord and realize His purpose of
_____ _____ _____ for the Lord. What else can we learn from John's story?

We have a deep, _____ _____ for salvation, and we require someone bold to tell us the _____. Truth is love.

Luke 3:7-9

Sometimes in the story of our lives, we have characters who are _____ _____ _____. Give them reason to say, "Thank you for never giving up on me."

We need to ask for _____ and _____ and _____ _____ _____ friends and family. The boldness to share must live inside us as believers.

Matthew 11:2-6

DISCUSS

How would you want to be approached with the good news of Jesus?

Is there someone in your life you have been supporting for a very long time, with no change, and you need encouragement to keep on keeping on?

Video downloads of this session are available for purchase at *www.lifeway.com/karenkingsbury*

If you are on social media, share what you are learning *#familyofjesus*

STUDY

LEGACY AND PURPOSE

A knowing filled John. This whole journey was about Jesus, about preparing people for Jesus. Telling them about Him. His cousin, his best friend. The pieces didn't quite fit together yet. But they would one day soon. And when they did, John knew this much for sure: Jesus would be at the center of it all.

THE FAMILY OF JESUS, *page 70*

. . . .

He closed his eyes and he was there again …

He was eight and nine and ten and he and his parents were welcoming Jesus and His family at the Passover and he and Jesus were running down the street, racing and gathering all the kids in the village to play together. He could see Jesus's eyes. The kindest, most sincere eyes anyone could ever have. His cousin, his best friend.

John breathed in deep. The smell of warm bread filled his senses and he was in the kitchen again, eleven years old, watching his mother bake. And she was telling him that he had to be careful with the yeast. A little yeast would work its way through the whole loaf of bread.

THE FAMILY OF JESUS, *page 93*

What a legacy of faithfulness! From the very beginning Elizabeth and Zechariah knew God's hand was on John, that He had a unique purpose. Filled with the Holy Spirit even as a child, John could discern right from wrong. His family taught and nurtured him, getting him ready to leave so he could prepare the way for Someone else.

What memories come to mind of your tapestry of faith?

What faith experiences do you want your own children to have? Your family? Your friends?

How has God been preparing you to fulfill your calling?

Growing up. Learning from the rabbis and soaking up the Torah teachings. Waiting to be ready when God did speak. For John, waiting preceded ministry.

John's waiting took place in the wilderness of the desert. In its quiet solitude, he listened for God. He pondered just as his parents reflected on God's activity. John had an unusual, distinctive approach to defining his ministry.

> *John was twenty-two now, and his purpose had never been more pressing in his heart. His time at the school had been well spent: learning every day, but listening, too. So much listening. Sometimes he would spend days in the desert by himself, just listening in silence, sleeping on the sandy ground under the stars, pondering the mystery of God's love for His people. Still, John loved the fact that twice a year he got to go home.*
>
> *His pack held a flask of water and some basic food. John's diet had changed since he'd been training for God. He could survive on very little now—whatever he could harvest from the desert floor. Locusts mostly. And honey from the comb ...*
>
> *"See you in a week." John nodded to the rabbi.*
>
> *"Look for God in the journey." His teacher's eyes narrowed, full of wisdom. "Even when you are away from school, the Father is teaching. Be listening."*
>
> THE FAMILY OF JESUS, *pages 70-71*

What role has God given you at this season of your life? Where do waiting and listening fit in?

Read Jeremiah 1:5; Mark 10:44-45; and Ephesians 1:18.

What perspectives about calling do these verses provide?

No one's calling is exactly the same as another person's. While John went into the desert, his cousin Jesus did not; the Father gave Jesus a different mission and setting.

Christians are called to be set apart from the world, but we are not all called to separate ourselves from culture, as John did. We have been created with deep ingenuity, and are meant to live creatively and purposefully.

> *The calling came a month after John's thirtieth birthday. He was studying in the desert, memorizing Scripture, and waiting on the Lord when he heard the voice. John wasn't sure if he heard it in his heart or if the voice boomed across the barren desert floor. But the message was clear: John needed to go to the countryside around the Jordan River and baptize people, burying them in water and raising them up out of it to a new life, a new understanding of God.*
>
> THE FAMILY OF JESUS, *page 75*

When have you heard God speaking to you so clearly?

Read Isaiah 40:3–5 and Luke 3:3–6.

What do these verses tell you about an Old Testament prophecy and its fulfillment?

> *Suddenly in a burst of clarity John understood. The prophet that Isaiah had been talking about was John himself! Zechariah and Elizabeth's only son—of all people. He wasn't just preparing the way for the people near the Jordan River. According to the prophet, he would prepare the way for all people. Everywhere.*
>
> THE FAMILY OF JESUS, *page 76*

As he began teaching and pointing people to the coming Messiah, John attacked sin and called for repentance. John's demeanor was strident and convicting; his appearance and diet, unusual. He passionately called people to repent and be baptized to show a change in direction.

John seemingly had no fear, even challenging religious and political leaders of hypocrisy and sin. Increasingly, he was drawing attention and getting questions.

MINISTRY AND QUESTIONS

Read Luke 3:15 to find out what people were asking themselves about John.

Read John 1:19—20 for how he answered them.

Based on Mark 1:7-8, how did John clarify his role?

Similar questions were coming to John's cousin Jesus. When Jesus came to him one day to be baptized, John was privileged to witness a defining moment.

Read Psalm 2:7 and Matthew 3:13—17.

Who brought this prophecy to completion? When and where?

"The Father's words at Jesus' baptism blend together two important Old Testament texts: Psalm 2 and Isaiah 42:1 Psalm 2 was a song sung at the crowning of Israel's kings. The Father's application of this text to Jesus identified Him as a divinely appointed King who would rule with divine authority and whose kingdom would extend to the ends of the earth (Ps. 2:1-12). The illusion to Isaiah 42 identified Jesus as the Servant, whom Isaiah 53:5 promised would be 'pierced because of our transgressions, crushed because of our iniquities.'"[6]

The wording in Matthew is one of only a few occasions in Scripture in which all three persons of the Trinity are present in one verse or passage (see also Matt. 28:19; 2 Cor. 13:13). Jesus' baptism and the subsequent heavenly declaration provided confirmation of Jesus' divinity, validated John the Baptist's ministry, and launched Jesus' earthly ministry.

Jesus' own Father identified Him as His "beloved Son," in whom He took delight (see Matt. 3:17; Mark 1:11; 9:7). John must have been overjoyed to see Jesus launch His own ministry—and knowing He had been a part. It wouldn't be too long before John's own ministry as forerunner would be marked by uncertainty.

AFFIRMATION AND REWARD

It's hard to follow your call to completion when you are in some type of prison. Failure. Sin. Addiction. Life spiraling out of control. Unanswered questions.

Read Matthew 11:1–3.

What questions did John have?

Imprisonment was very real to John the Baptist, who had angered Herod by calling out the leader's adulterous relationship. Thrown into prison, John had only his thoughts and faith as company. It was hard not to have questions.

> *Yes, he still felt the presence of the Spirit. But his purpose no longer felt certain. What if he hadn't heard the Lord correctly? What if he should have waited another year before heading to the Jordan River? Maybe he'd been too anxious, too overzealous. By the time John heard the calling, he was full of a holy sort of anger at the sins of the people. He could hardly wait to show them the error of their ways and turn them back to God again.*
>
> *Maybe his approach had been wrong.*
>
> THE FAMILY OF JESUS, *pages 89-90*

Read Matthew 11:4–11 and 13:43–46.

How did Jesus answer John's questions?

"John was the hinge between the past age and the coming age. Jesus then used the greatness of John to contrast the surpassing greatness of the kingdom of heaven. Just as the greatest treasures on earth paled in comparison with the prize of the kingdom, even so John, as wonderful as he was, paled in comparison to the least significant member of the kingdom."[7]

John's tears came again.

Jesus cared about him. He hadn't forgotten His cousin sitting in a prison cell. The comfort John gleaned from those words made him feel as if Jesus had stepped into the dank cell and hugged him the way He had at the Jordan River. Jesus was the Messiah. John had played his part and prepared the way, whatever happened from this point on …

"Time's up, John the Baptist!" The three of them laughed, much louder than before. "No more preaching for you!"

More words came from their mouths, but John could no longer hear them. The sounds and smells changed, and he could feel the sun on his shoulders. He remembered the Scriptures, the promises of God. A joyful life lay just ahead. The least in the kingdom of heaven would be greater than anyone on earth. John smiled.

He could hardly wait.

THE FAMILY OF JESUS, *pages 96-97*

LIVING IN GOD'S STORY

GOING DEEPER

Home study can help you better understand God's work in John the Baptist's life—and in your own. You may want to read more of the biblical narrative, in Matthew 3; 11; 14:1-12; Mark 1:1-11; Luke 1; 3; John 1; 5:31-36. For more insights about John the Baptist in The Family of Jesus, *read chapter 3 (pp. 69-98).*

In learning to love Jesus more by studying the people who knew Him best, you can also discover principles for relating to your family. Use this unique opportunity to build a stronger home as you learn more about Jesus and His family.

DAY 1

PRACTICE AFFIRMATION

When asked about His cousin (see Matt. 11:7-11), Jesus affirmed the special role of John the Baptist. Jesus' words gave John great comfort and joy.

While Jesus' affirmation was unique—He was affirming John's role in the kingdom and in His own mission—the impact of affirmation cannot be overlooked.

This week look for something you can affirm in someone. Try to do this exercise every day. Be sincere, speaking truthfully, and watch to see what difference this makes for you and the other person. Be ready to share some responses with your group.

Did looking for something to affirm in an individual in any way change your opinion of this person?

Did it become easier to be an encourager as you practiced affirmation?

Search the number of times the word "encourage" (or similar word depending on translation) appears in the New Testament. Record what you discovered.

What does this tell you about what believers should be doing?

Read Philippians 2:1—3.

"If then there is any encouragement in Christ, if any consolation of love, if any fellowship with the Spirit, if any affection and mercy, fulfill my joy by thinking the same way, having the same love, sharing the same feelings, focusing on one goal. Do nothing out of rivalry or conceit, but in humility consider others as more important than yourselves."

DAY 2
TEACHING REPENTANCE

The crowds grew larger. After hundreds of years of silence, they wondered if John might be the Christ.

When he got word of this, he held up his hands and waited until he had the attention of the crowd. "I baptize you with water. But One who is more powerful than I am will come." He looked at the faces gathered at the river. "I'm not good enough to untie the straps of His sandals. He will baptize you with the Holy Spirit and with fire. His pitchfork is in His hand to toss the straw away from the threshing floor."

The people moved in closer, gripped by John's words. "He will gather the wheat into His storeroom. But He will burn up the husks with fire that can't be put out."

The people understood he was talking about them. They needed to repent of their sins, they needed forgiveness, or they would be cut off from God. And so people came by the hundreds so John could baptize them.

THE FAMILY OF JESUS, *page 78*

Read Matthew 3:1–36; Mark 1:2–3; and Luke 3:3–4.

What do you learn from these verses about John the Baptist and his calling?

What exactly does it mean to "prepare the way"?

Read Luke 3:4–6.

John the Baptist was creating a favorable environment and making it easy for Jesus to enter into the lives of the people. John's purpose was to call the people to repent of their sin and be baptized.

Why would these two outcomes be so important in preparation for the Lord?

Unconfessed sin hinders us from seeing the Lord and staying in a right relationship with Him.

What do these verses tell you about repentance of sins? Circle the words *sin*, *confess our sins*, and *transgressions* every time you see them. Underline the results of repentance of sins.

But if we walk in the light as He Himself is in the light, we have fellowship with one another, and the blood of Jesus His Son cleanses us from all sin. If we say, "We have no sin," we are deceiving ourselves, and the truth is not in us. If we confess our sins, He is faithful and righteous to forgive us our sins and to cleanse us from all unrighteousness.
1 JOHN 1:7-9

As far as the east is from the west, so far has He removed our transgressions from us.
PSALM 103:12

The one who conceals his sins will not prosper, but whoever confesses and renounces them will find mercy.
PROVERBS 28:13

When we confess our sin and receive forgiveness through Jesus Christ we prepare the way for Him to operate in our lives. John also baptized those who repented of their sins. He baptized with water as an outward demonstration of a person's repentance from sin and commitment to God. Today, baptism is a symbol of our identification with Christ. It illustrates Christ's burial and resurrection and our new life with Him.

Take time to jot down a few of your thoughts about John's teaching.

Pray, asking the Lord to open your heart to Him without pride, shame, or embarrassment. Maybe there are some things you need to confess today. Ask Jesus for the forgiveness that only He can give.

MAKING THE MOST OF TIME

We have one life. What are we going to do with it? How do we make the most of the time God has allotted to us?

The Greek word *kairos* means time. But not just minutes, seconds, hours, clocks, or sundials. *Kairos* is about the flow of time or a specific measurement of time. It carries the idea of the finding or placement of the right time, of a predetermined time or the opportune time. No matter whether you are talking about the time when you get moving or the appointed, proper time to take advantage of an opportunity, eventually *kairos* is going to slip away.

John the Baptist found himself in the midst of a tug-of-war with time. He knew he had a calling on his life and needed to help prepare the people for the Messiah.

Read Philippians 3:10—14.

What does it mean to know Jesus and "the power of His resurrection"?

When Jesus has taken hold of your life, how do you live? How do you make the most of your time for His kingdom, for His plans, and for His purposes?

How might sufferings and the resurrection power of Jesus connect based on these verses?

Read Ephesians 5:15—17.

Pay careful attention, then, to how you walk—not as unwise people but as wise—making the most of the time, because the days are evil. So don't be foolish, but understand what the Lord's will is.

Read Colossians 4:5.

Act wisely toward outsiders, making the most of the time.

In each of these verses the writer reminds up to make the most of the time.

What do you gain from reading these verses?

How might taking these verses to heart influence how you spend your time?

WHEN CRISES OF FAITH COME

John walked across his darkened prison cell and gripped the bars. But what about him? He and Jesus were supposed to work together ... And now when the time had finally come to prepare the way, to tell the world the truth about Jesus and salvation, John was stuck in this wretched hole.

THE FAMILY OF JESUS, *page 85*

John had lived his life faithful to his calling. He had lived in the wilderness and baptized others after they repented of their sins. He was in the middle of his mission; yet, he found himself in prison for doing exactly what God had called him to do. He was obedient. He was faithful. He believed. So why was this happening?

Crisis of faith. It is what we think of when someone experiences an internal conflict or intense doubt in his or her beliefs. It is when you are shaken to the core and have to evaluate why you believe what you believe and if you truly believe it. Have you ever been there? Like John, maybe you have wondered why:

- You have been faithful in your marriage, but your husband is unfaithful.

- You have given everything you have to your children, and one of them pulls away and wants nothing to do with you.

- You are committed to your job and one day you are given a pink slip and asked to pack your things.

- You have cared, listened, and been a friend; yet you are shut out of her life.

Look at some examples of people in the Bible who experienced a crisis of faith.

WHO	SCRIPTURE	CRISIS DESCRIPTION
Abraham	Genesis 22:1-14	
Gideon	Judges 6:11-13	
Elijah	1 Kings 19:4-14	
Peter	Matthew 26:69-74	
Thomas	John 20:24-29	

Yes, we can relate to John the Baptist and many others in the Bible as they struggled with fears, doubt, disappointments, sadness, and heartache. Like us, they were trying to live out their faith and stand up for what they believed.

Read Matthew 11:1–11.

> *"As I was leaving, I heard Jesus talking to the crowd about you. So I stopped and listened. You should know what He said ... Jesus told them no one better than John the Baptist had ever been born. But even then, the least person in the kingdom of heaven is greater than you, John. Heaven is more important."*
>
> *The comfort John gleaned from those words made him feel as if Jesus had stepped into the dank cell and hugged him the way He had at the Jordan River. Jesus was the Messiah.*
>
> THE FAMILY OF JESUS, *pages 95-96*

Jesus did not forget about John when he needed confirmation and encouragement—and He will not forget about you. Pray for peace and assurance in your relationship with Him. If you still struggle, consider talking with your pastor, Bible teacher, or other Christian friend who can encourage you from Scripture.

SAYING NO SO YOU CAN SAY YES

"When will you be home for good?"

John thought for a moment. "Whenever I've completed the task God has for me." He didn't want to explain his role in preparing the way for the Messiah. "God is speaking to me in the desert. When it's time, He'll let me know."

"Whenever that is ... when you're finished with that task ... then will you come home?"

Again John let her [Anne's] words run through his heart. "Yes." He felt a ripple of joy start inside and make its way to his face. "Yes, when I've finished the work God has for me, I'll come home"

THE FAMILY OF JESUS, *pages 73-74*

When have you made sacrifices for the benefit of others?

What are some examples of times when you gave up doing something good so that you could pursue what was best? How difficult was it to say no to some things in order to say yes to others?

What do you think John had to give up in order to fulfill the task and calling God had on his life?

If we are not careful we can overextend ourselves. We can commit to so many good things that we end up feeling like we are not good at anything.

Do you find that your to-do list never ends? Is there any margin for error if your schedule is delayed?

John moved to the desert and did what he was called to do. Our world seem to be so very different. We have to learn to say no and to develop a filter on how to prioritize the times when we say yes. We can learn much from people in the Bible who were sold out to their task and calling.

Review these examples from Scripture.

SCRIPTURE	PERSON	CALLING/SACRIFICE
Matthew 3:3-5	John the Baptist	Prepare the way for the Messiah/Moved to the desert and ate locusts
1 Samuel 24	David	Would be king according to God's timing and as a man of integrity/ Would not kill to gain the throne
Esther 4	Queen Esther	To save the Jews from slaughter/Approaching the king unsummoned could mean death

What other examples from Scripture reveal the sacrifice that often accompanies calling?

How do you see this sacrifice lived out every day (military, teaching, parenting, acts of service, ministers, and others)?

Compare and contrast the number of yes's and no's you are making in your life. Use this chart to record the things you are answering to; it can reveal a lot about your choices.

NO	YES

What are some tasks or responsibilities for which it is time to say no?

What requests bring out the greatest gifts, talents, and passion in you and need to be "answered" with a yes?

John, it appears, never made it back home to Zechariah and Elizabeth. After the desert, he lived in a prison cell. He gave up a comfortable home, marriage, family, talking with friends in the marketplace, and any number of ways to make a living. Could he have lived a different life? Perhaps. But deep down he would have known he had accepted the good rather than the best. As he made the necessary sacrifices, John chose what was best.

In the end, John finished the work God had for him and finally went to his true home.

ELIZABETH: HOLDING OUT HOPE

John had indeed been freed from prison, and she would certainly see him again.

Just not the way she had planned.

The weight of his loss was still so heavy on her shoulders, in her heart. But for the first time since Herod's men had killed John, Elizabeth felt the stirrings of hope. God didn't always answer prayers the way His people expected. The way they intended.

Clearly, Elizabeth wanted John released from prison here, wanted him back home in the kitchen where he could tell her about his time with Jesus, and the lonely days behind bars. But she couldn't argue with the fact that her prayers had been answered.

THE FAMILY OF JESUS, *pages 109-110*

Hope endures. When prayers are constant. Hope endures. When dreams seem to go unfulfilled. God has not forgotten or forsaken.

"And consider your relative Elizabeth—even she has conceived a son in her old age, and this is the sixth month for her who was called childless. For nothing will be impossible with God" (Luke 1:36-37).

YOUR STORY

START

Everyone has a story. Enjoy sharing yours and hearing from your group as together you learn about another person in the family of Jesus—Elizabeth.

What is something your parents expected you to do when you were young?

Based on your study last week, share:

What did it feel like to be an intentional encourager this week? (day 1)

What do you think is the connection between sacrifice and calling? (day 5)

In looking ahead to Elizabeth's part of the story, discuss:

How has a parent, mentor, or trusted friend helped make your path smoother?

Why is it important to be able to say good-bye in some relationships? Where did that custom originate?

ELIZABETH'S STORY

WATCH

Watch Elizabeth's story from The Family of Jesus Bible Study DVD *and discuss the questions with your group.*

Elizabeth was always there for people—the birth coach, the babysitter, the mentor, the friend. But who was there for her? She leaned on the Lord. What can we learn from the story of Elizabeth?

Whatever your title, you are called to _____. Someone is hoping you will be the _____ she is looking for.

Elizabeth had to wait _____ before her prayer was answered.

Luke 1:23-25 ("The Lord has done this for me," v. 25).

Sometimes we just need a quiet season with the Lord to _____ _____ for what He is doing.

Our world is _____ _____ for someone to follow.

Luke 1:43-45

DISCUSS

How does it help you to know that there can be purpose in pain or suffering?

Is there something for which you waited much longer than you ever imagined? How much do you value it now?

Video downloads of this session are available for purchase at www.lifeway.com/karenkingsbury
If you are on social media, share what you are learning #familyofjesus

STVDY

WHEN PAIN HAS PURPOSE

The failure to be blessed with a child was shameful in Elizabeth and Zechariah's culture; note how in Luke 1:25, Elizabeth refers to her "disgrace." She was shunned by her neighbors, though her barrenness was not caused by sin. Instead, both she and Zechariah were "righteous in God's sight" and "living without blame" (Luke 1:6-7). This elderly couple was known for their faith and priestly service.

Elizabeth was well past child-bearing age. Yet, God would take her burden and turn it into a blessing.

How did God use these childless women in His redemptive plan?

- Sarah (Gen. 18:11-14)

- Rebekah (Gen. 25:21-24)

- Hannah (1 Sam. 1:1–2:1-11)

Like Elizabeth, have you ever been in a dark place, when you felt rejected? How did God answer your prayers and teach you something?

How has the body of Christ helped you through a painful time?

Pain often has purpose—a reality many of us see more clearly after the fact, even when we walk by faith. We live in a fallen world, which, by virtue of our sinful nature, is marked by violence, broken relationships, natural disasters, illness, and other distress caused by failure to live up to God's standards.

Circumstances don't always go according to our plans. The unexpected can draw us closer to God, help us focus on what matters most, and shape us into grateful people.

Read Luke 1:5–7, 24–25, 36–43.

In the days of King Herod of Judea, there was a priest of Abijah's division named Zechariah. His wife was from the daughters of Aaron, and her name was Elizabeth. Both were righteous in God's sight, living without blame according to all the commands and requirements of the Lord. But they had no children because Elizabeth could not conceive, and both of them were well along in years.

· ·

After these days his wife Elizabeth conceived and kept herself in seclusion for five months. She said, "The Lord has done this for me. He has looked with favor in these days to take away my disgrace among the people."

· ·

"And consider your relative Elizabeth—even she has conceived a son in her old age, and this is the sixth month for her who was called childless. For nothing will be impossible with God."

"I am the Lord's slave," said Mary. "May it be done to me according to your word." Then the angel left her.

In those days Mary set out and hurried to a town in the hill country of Judah where she entered Zechariah's house and greeted Elizabeth. When Elizabeth heard Mary's greeting, the baby leaped inside her, and Elizabeth was filled with the Holy Spirit. Then she exclaimed with a loud cry:

"You are the most blessed of women, and your child will be blessed! How could this happen to me, that the mother of my Lord should come to me?"

Based on this passage, how did Elizabeth's loss and shame end in healing?

After a long period of silence, in the time of Herod the Great, God acted to reveal His redemption. While He was moving to fulfill His promises to Israel, God also responded to the needs of a righteous couple, Elizabeth and Zechariah.

It was time to present little John and then—only then—could Zechariah speak ... "His name is John! His name has to be John!" From that day on everyone knew what Elizabeth and Zechariah had known from the beginning: God's hand was on their son. He was special. Filled with the Holy Spirit. The angel had said that, and the proof was evident.

THE FAMILY OF JESUS, *page 105*

For what things do you think Elizabeth was especially grateful?

Her husband could speak again! Not only that, Zechariah also sang—prophetically.

Read Luke 1:67–79.

Place yourself in the room with the people who heard Zechariah's song. What thoughts might they have had? What emotions might they have experienced?

The sounds quieted and she felt herself remembering a happier time. Zechariah had just found his voice and people were celebrating the miracle. And Zechariah began to praise their mighty God, the One who had given them a child in their later years. And Zechariah was singing. After nine months of silence he was singing a song that had been growing in his heart the whole time. ...

She could only beg God in the quiet, desperate places of her soul that the last line of Zechariah's song might also be true. That peace might come because of God's kindness.

THE FAMILY OF JESUS, *pages 107-108*

How does the idea of God's kindness encourage you?

Describe a time when you knew without a doubt that you were in the presence of God.

Read Luke 1:39–45.

Inspired by the Holy Spirit, Elizabeth rejoiced in Mary's blessing.

Why do you think Elizabeth expressed such joy at God's blessing in Mary's life?

Sometimes it is difficult to celebrate the good things that happen to other people, especially when our lives have been marked by disappointment. Cultivating a grateful heart opens us to the many good gifts God gives—and wants to give—us. In this case, the Holy Spirit enabled Elizabeth to recognize that her son John would be a vital part of Jesus' purpose and ministry.

Both women were encouragers, helping each other. Their lives were intertwined by their unique call as well as by their relationship as cousins. They would continue to learn from each other about what to expect next as God's story unfolded.

MORE EYES TURNING TO JESUS

Read Mark 6:1–6 to learn about Jesus' early ministry in His hometown.

What were people in Nazareth saying about Him?

What were they wondering about Him (look ahead to vv. 14-15)?

Read Mark 6:16—29.

What part did Herod and Herodias play in John the Baptist's story?

"Elizabeth ... are you okay?" It was Zechariah's voice. "Please open your eyes."

Only she didn't want to open her eyes because then it would be real again. Even with her eyes closed she remembered what had happened. John had been killed in prison. Her firstborn. Her only child. Her son. He was gone now.

THE FAMILY OF JESUS, *page 106*

Elizabeth had lived too long, long enough to see an angry reaction and political maneuvering in respond to John's wilderness preaching for repentance. Long enough for her firstborn to be imprisoned and brutally murdered. Heaven seemed very inviting now. Even now, as raw as the pain was, Elizabeth was beginning to see a bigger picture through her tears, with the help of dear Mary.

"Jesus could've rescued John. He could've gotten him out of prison or brought him back to life. We both know that." Mary's voice trembled. "But something bigger is happening. It's something Simeon said at the end of our brief moment with him. That's the part I haven't wanted to think about."

THE FAMILY OF JESUS, *page 113*

Read Luke 2:25–35.

What do you think Simeon meant when he told Mary "a sword will pierce your own soul" (v. 35)?

Tears welled in Mary's eyes again. "I was thinking about what Simeon said, all those years ago. How I would have pain, too." She hung her head for a moment, struggling to finish. "[Elizabeth,] you showed me how to bring my baby into the world. What if … what if you are supposed to show me how to let Him go?" …

The rest of the day and long after Mary left, the conversation replayed in [Elizabeth's] mind. It left her feeling lighter, more hopeful. Anxious for heaven. Because maybe Mary was right about Elizabeth's heartache. Her pain was not without purpose. God had chosen her to prepare the way for Mary in birth.

Now, just maybe, He had chosen her to prepare the way in death.

THE FAMILY OF JESUS, *pages 116-117*

What would you tell someone about Elizabeth's part in God's story?

LIVING IN GOD'S STORY

GOING DEEPER

Home study can help you better understand God's work in Elizabeth's life—and in your own. For more insights about Elizabeth in The Family of Jesus, *read chapter 4 (pp. 99-120).*

In learning to love Jesus more by studying the people who knew Him best, you can also discover principles for relating to your family. Use this unique opportunity to build a stronger home as you learn more about Jesus and His family.

DAY 1

PREPARING THE WAY

How are you preparing the way for others? Pointing people to Jesus?

In our DVD teaching, Elizabeth is described as a mentor, a trusted counselor or guide. According to *Merriam-Webster's Dictionary*, a *mentor* is "someone who teaches or gives help and advice to a less experienced and often younger person, to tutor."[8] A mentor requires a mentee, a protégé or someone who is willing and available to be tutored. A trusting relationship that allows for teaching, accountability, openness, and sharing makes mentoring a rich experience.

A good example is an intern being mentored by an experienced surgeon. In daily, hands-on, safe surgical situations he or she learns what is needed to save lives through appropriate surgical procedures.

While the word *mentoring* is not used in the Bible, mentoring relationships and spiritual leadership are clearly evident. Moses learned from his father-in-law how to do his work. Jesus both taught and led by example as He mentored the disciples. Paul's development of Timothy is another example. A godly woman who reaches out to other women to help them know the way she has taken is a mentor. A woman who willingly chooses to benefit from someone else's faith experiences is a mentee.

The ways Mary and Elizabeth interacted reveal benefits of mentoring. When the people involved are focused on obeying God, mentoring relationships promote spiritual growth.

Identify some spiritual mentors and how they influenced you.

Mary measured out the flour and yeast. "I taught Jesus about the yeast." Mary smiled. "Just as you taught me back then." Her eyes met Elizabeth's. "Jesus used what I taught Him in His teaching to the people. I think about it whenever I make bread."

"What does He teach about it?" Elizabeth welcomed the distraction, the chance to talk about something other than John's death.

"He compares the yeast to false teaching. It doesn't take much to ruin faith."
THE FAMILY OF JESUS, *page 111*

Being a mentor may be as simple as making bread or sharing a meal together. It may be reflected in younger women spending time with older, trusted women who are willing to pour into them. Younger women want to know: What's it like to be a mother? How can I learn from you? What is it like to follow Jesus? Will you teach me what you know?

With whom would you like to "make bread" or share life? Do the two of you already have a relationship? Have you talked about taking this further? Have you ever thought about mentoring someone yourself?

Read 2 Timothy 1:3–5.

Paul highlights for Timothy a successful example of equipping the future generation—one Timothy certainly recognized. Both his grandmother, Lois, and his mother, Eunice, introduced him to God at an early age, and Paul recognized the same faith in him—and was willing to pour his life into Timothy's. Sounds like several good examples of mentoring to me.

CAPABLE WIFE AND MOTHER

> *Elizabeth returned to the basin in the kitchen. The olives still needed pressing. She began working on them, the way she'd done a thousand times. God had blessed them with old age—a gift many couples didn't get. But at this point, heaven wasn't far off for either of them. Elizabeth wanted only to live long enough to see John again, to see him freed from the prison cell. To that end, she prayed constantly.*
>
> THE FAMILY OF JESUS, *page 100*

Luke 1:5-6 provides high praise for Zechariah and Elizabeth: "*both* were righteous, not just one of them; *both* lived "without blame" (HCSB, italics added); *both* were "righteous in the sight of God" (NIV), "walking blamelessly in *all* the commandments and requirements of the Lord" (AMP, italics added). No doubt righteous living extended to their marriage and to their parenting of long-awaited John.

Several passages from Proverbs give us a feel for what a wife like Elizabeth looks like:

> A capable wife is her husband's crown, but a wife who causes shame is like rottenness in his bones (12:4).

> A man who finds a wife finds a good thing and obtains favor from the LORD (18:22).

> Who can find a capable wife? She is far more precious than jewels. The heart of her husband trusts in her, and he will not lack anything good. She rewards him with good, not evil, all the days of her life (31:10-12).

Read Proverbs 20:6—7 for the kind of man she served.

> Many a man proclaims his own loyalty, but who can find a trustworthy man? The one who lives with integrity is righteous; his children who come after him will be happy.

We see how Elizabeth loved sitting down with Mary and encouraging her, how they supported each other at critical times. We can imagine how Elizabeth likely interacted with other young mothers in her community.

Elizabeth and Hannah shared some common issues in their respective journeys. Can you picture what it would have been like for them to have shared a meal and a conversation? If you haven't already done so in the group session, read 1 Samuel 1:1–2:11 for Hannah's background.

What burden did Hannah carry (1:5-7)? What did she do about it (1:10-11)? What happened, according to verses 19-20?

What similarities do you see in John the Baptist's birth (see Luke 1:5-25,57-66; also refer to 1 Sam. 2:1-11)?

What commitment did Hannah act on in 1 Samuel 1:24-28? What principle does she affirm for you?

Children belong to the Lord, who graciously gives them to parents. Hannah physically gave Samuel back to the Lord to serve Him. In a similar way, Elizabeth and Zechariah knew before John was born that they would ultimately release him back to God to fulfill His purpose. Surely, they were motivated to be the best parents they could be.

If you are a mother, how do you view parenting and your children?

Here are some biblical reminders about the joys and responsibilities God has entrusted to parents. Choose one passage as your prayer of commitment: Exodus 20:12; Deuteronomy 6:6-9; Psalm 127; Proverbs 1:8-9; 22:6; Ephesians 6:1-4; 2 Timothy 3:14-15.

INEXPLICABLE BURDENS AND AMAZING ANSWERS

We know from Scripture that Elizabeth was a righteous woman who had found favor with God. For a long time, she had carried the burden of childlessness. Her shame may have spilled over to how people related to Zechariah.

> From Psalm 31:11; 41:9; 88:8,18, identify some of the emotions David felt at a similar time in his life.

David felt even more alone without the support of his neighbors and friends. Being isolated can make a hard situation even worse.

Read Genesis 15:1–6.

> How did this situation compare to Elizabeth's? How did God describe Abraham in verse 6?

Elizabeth, no doubt, was driven even closer to God for His comfort, promises, and presence. We, too, can know through His Word that God will speak to us in our suffering and will show Himself strong when we are weak.

> Even when I go through the darkest valley, I fear no danger, for You are with me; Your rod and Your staff—they comfort me (Ps. 23:4).

> My soul, praise the LORD, and do not forget all His benefits. He forgives all your sin; He heals all your diseases. He redeems your life from the Pit; He crowns you with faithful love and compassion (Ps. 103:2-4).

Do not fear, for I am with you; do not be afraid, for I am your God. I will strengthen you; I will help you; I will hold on to you with My righteous right hand (Isa. 41:10).

He comforts us in all our affliction, so that we may be able to comfort those who are in any kind of affliction, through the comfort we ourselves receive from God. For as the sufferings of Christ overflow to us, so through Christ our comfort also overflows (2 Cor. 1:4-5).

May our Lord Jesus Christ Himself and God our Father, who has loved us and given us eternal encouragement and good hope by grace, encourage your hearts and strengthen you in every good work and word (2 Thess. 2:16-17).

For God has not given us a spirit of fearfulness, but one of power, love, and sound judgment (2 Tim. 1:7).

Sometimes suffering is a judgment on or outcome of sin. God has imposed suffering on entire nations to draw people back to Him. There are times when pain or suffering seems inexplicable, especially when a righteous person is the focus.

Almost always, we are shaped into better ministers as we work with God through our pain. Scripture acknowledges Elizabeth's faithfulness, so we can assume that she ministered to others even as she was working through her own sorrow.

Who do you know who has been carrying a burden for a long time?

What ongoing ministry opportunities are needed? How is your very presence and support a ministry?

Read Genesis 15:1–6 and Luke 1:57.

How did God answer both Abraham and Elizabeth, according to His timing and plan?

DAY 4

BLESSINGS UNDESERVED

Generally, everyone we have met in Jesus' family has reason to acknowledge gracious and undeserved blessings. Patient Elizabeth—humble and prayerful—set an example of thankfulness to others.

Use this time to reflect on the goodness of God. Unpack Scriptures about grace, mercy, and thankfulness—all of which only begin to capture God's undeserved blessing on our lives. Spend time thanking Him, praising Him, soaking it all in, and making some new commitments.

Read Psalm 84:11—12.

Identify the ways God gives grace and glory.

Read John 1:17.

How has grace trumped striving and effort for you?

Read 2 Corinthians 8:9.

Describe the riches you have in Jesus Christ.

Read 2 Corinthians 9:8; Ephesians 3:20–21; Hebrews 4:16.

How has He shown Himself able beyond your expectations?

Read Romans 11:33–36.

> Oh, the depth of the riches
> both of the wisdom and the knowledge of God!
> How unsearchable His judgments
> and untraceable His ways!
> For who has known the mind of the Lord?
> Or who has been His counselor?
> Or who has ever first given to Him,
> and has to be repaid?
> For from Him and through Him
> and to Him are all things.
> To Him be the glory forever. Amen.

How can you glorify God in your life today?

ALL EYES ON JESUS

What does it mean to help other people turn their eyes toward Jesus?
What part could your story play?

Read John 4:25–30; 39–42.

What did the woman do after believing in Jesus?

Many in Samaria became believers because of the woman's testimony about Jesus. "The woman at the well experienced the freedom that only Christ can give. Today He offers wounded women the same freedom from self, prejudice, and sin. That is true hope for a hurting world."[9]

With all the different worldviews drawing attention today, what does it mean to focus our eyes on Jesus and Him alone?

"It doesn't take much to ruin faith" (p. 85) may very well refer to some of the dangers of false teachings.

Read Matthew 23:1–13.

What did Jesus have to say about false teachings and hypocrisy?
What did He commend instead?

The religious leaders were turning people away from God rather than toward Him. By their restrictions the scribes and the Pharisees made faith burdensome. Jesus left no doubt about where He stood: "Woe to you, scribes and Pharisees, hypocrites!" (v. 13), modeling servanthood instead. The religious leaders grieved Him, just as they had grieved John the Baptist when he was preaching repentance in the desert.

Similarly, when our actions do not match our expressed allegiance to Jesus or the words we speak, the people who watch us can turn away. When we model love and servanthood instead, out of our love for God, untold opportunities become available.

The apostle Paul had words of caution and encouragement for believers who face attempts to add to the gospel or take away vital truths.

Read 2 Timothy 3:13–17.

> Evil people and impostors will become worse, deceiving and being deceived. But as for you, continue in what you have learned and firmly believed. You know those who taught you, and you know that from childhood you have known the sacred Scriptures, which are able to give you wisdom for salvation through faith in Christ Jesus. All Scripture is inspired by God and is profitable for teaching, for rebuking, for correcting, for training in righteousness, so that the man of God may be complete, equipped for every good work.

We are to be careful as we teach those in our own household, for children take their faith to the next generation. Being grounded in faith early gives them wisdom for salvation and a foundation. We must exercise care not to "ruin" our faith or that of our family by focusing on wrong or lesser things.

Read 1 Thessalonians 5:21–22.

> Test all things. Hold on to what is good. Stay away from every kind of evil.

As much as people resist hearing there is only one way to anything, there *is* only one way to reconciliation with God. Jesus showed us by living a sinless life among us and He told us: "I am the way, the truth, and the life" (John 14:6). While others through the centuries have made similar claims, Jesus alone can be trusted because of who He is: God incarnate, fully human, and fully divine. He can be trusted because of what He did—live a sinless life to show us God, die a sacrificial death on our behalf, and conquer death and sin because He is alive and will live forever. No one else can make the claim to be the only way to God. We are to focus our eyes and hearts on Him.

JAMES: FROM SKEPTICISM TO COMMITMENT

All of Nazareth was in an uproar and James was sick of it. His brother was acting insane so maybe it was time to take action. James stepped outside his house and leaned against the doorframe.

Jesus was having dinner down the street and even from this distance James could see the multitudes, gathering around the dwelling, pushing their way inside.

"Jesus! Help us ... Jesus, over here! Jesus, heal us!"

James watched through wary eyes.

THE FAMILY OF JESUS, *page 121*

Now if any of you lacks wisdom, he should ask God, who gives to all generously and without criticizing, and it will be given to him. But let him ask in faith without doubting. For the doubter is like the surging sea, driven and tossed by the wind. That person should not expect to receive anything from the Lord. An indecisive man is unstable in all his ways.
—James 1:5-8

YOUR STORY

START

Everyone has a story. Enjoy sharing yours and hearing from your group as together you learn about another person in the family of Jesus—James.

Based on your study last week, talk together about:

How has grace trumped striving and effort for you? (day 4)

How can your very presence be a ministry to someone? What steps have you decided to take to act ? (day 3)

In thinking about James, Jesus' half brother, share:

What examples of sibling rivalry come to mind from your childhood?

If you lived in Jerusalem and James was your pastor or neighbor, what would you like to ask him about his time with Jesus?

JAMES'S STORY

WATCH

Watch James's story from The Family of Jesus Bible Study DVD *and discuss the question with your group.*

James thought his big brother could _____ _____ _____—until Jesus actually did. What can we learn from the story of James?

The one who had rushed the house where Jesus was teaching, telling people Jesus was out of His mind, would later record that everyone should be _____ and slow to speak, slow to become angry (see Jas. 1:19).

Mark 3:20-21,31-35

Jesus wanted James to know that the _____ _____ were the ones who would believe in Him. And it is still that way.

James was also aware that although he had been humiliated by Jesus, he was _____.

1 Corinthians 15:7-8

James 1:27

DISCUSS

How does God find ways to use us despite our regrets and failures?

Video downloads of this session are available for purchase at *www.lifeway.com/karenkingsbury*

If you are on social media, share what you are learning *#familyofjesus*

STVDY

CRAZY BIG BROTHER?

> *What was Jesus trying to prove? James had figured someday soon Jesus would be His old self, and they could go on being a family: Making memories and sharing meals. Working in the shop. James and his best friend, Jesus. His big brother.*
>
> THE FAMILY OF JESUS, *pages 128-129*

Read Mark 3:20–21.

> Then He [Jesus] went home, and the crowd gathered again so that they were not even able to eat. When His family heard this, they set out to restrain Him, because they said, "He's out of His mind."

What are some descriptions people today give of Jesus?

A good man, a teacher, a liar, and a prophet are a few that come to mind. In Jesus' time, many were eagerly anticipating the Messiah who was to come.

> *For months Jesus had been traveling throughout the entire region, claiming to heal people and drive out demons. All sorts of nonsense. However He was pulling off the trickery, His actions were causing people to believe He was the Messiah.*
>
> THE FAMILY OF JESUS, *page 129*

Read John 7:1–5.

> After this, Jesus traveled in Galilee, since He did not want to travel in Judea because the Jews were trying to kill Him. The Jewish Festival of Tabernacles was near, so His brothers said to Him, "Leave here and go to Judea so Your disciples can see Your works that You are doing. For no one does anything in secret while he's seeking public recognition. If You do these things, show Yourself to the world." (For not even His brothers believed in Him.)

Which do you think would be easier—to believe in Jesus without seeing Him or to accept Him during His ministry on earth? Explain your thoughts.

Read Luke 5:15–26.

What truth about Himself did Jesus establish in verses 20-25?

How did the people respond (see v. 26)?

What does this truth mean to you?

A DIFFERENT MESSIAH

Jesus was a different type of Messiah than the one people were expecting. Do your own comparison of several Old Testament prophecies of the Messiah and some New Testament descriptions of Jesus.

PROPHECY: THE MESSIAH WOULD SPEAK IN PARABLES.

How do these Old Testament passages describe the coming Messiah?

- Psalm 78:2-4

- Isaiah 6:9-10

How does Matthew 13:10-15,34-35 describe Jesus?

PROPHECY: THE MESSIAH WOULD BE SENT TO HEAL THE BROKENHEARTED.

How does Isaiah 61:1-2 describe the coming Messiah?

How does Luke 4:15-22 describe Jesus?

PROPHECY: THE MESSIAH WOULD BE REJECTED BY HIS OWN PEOPLE.

How do these Old Testament passages describe the coming Messiah?

- Psalm 69:8

- Isaiah 53:3

How do John 1:9-10 and John 7:1-5 describe Jesus?

What do these descriptions tell you about Jesus?

Read Mark 6:3.

In what ways do you think Jesus' own family might have felt rejected by Jesus?

How do we sometimes miss out on the best in the people we know best—our family and close friends?

"He's the Messiah, no matter what anyone says."

James froze in place "What?"

Even in the noise of the crowd, his mother spoke loud enough to be heard. "He is the Messiah. I've known that since before He was born."

This was the final blow. "You've believed Him all along."

"Yes." His mother didn't break eye contact. "Even when I wanted to doubt Him to protect Him, I believed." …

One of Jesus's followers put his hand on Mary's shoulder. "We need to get to the road. Come on, Mary."

She nodded but kept her attention on James. "Are you coming?"

"No." He had to draw the line somewhere. "I am not one of His followers."

THE FAMILY OF JESUS, *pages 137-138*

Have you ever drawn the line in relation to following Jesus?

Do you know Him as Savior and Lord? If so, who introduced Jesus to you? If not, what is holding you back?

Where was the justice in all this? Jesus might've been mad, but He wasn't dangerous. He'd done nothing worthy of the death penalty. The small band of supporters moved quickly, pushing their way through the throng of people, but James stayed apart from the group. As in Jesus' life, the crowd was split—some wailed, begging the soldiers to have mercy. Others mocked Jesus, demanding His crucifixion.

This far from Nazareth no one recognized James moving along by himself, no one pointed and stared at him because he was related to Jesus. But as the crying around him grew, James was no longer sure he cared whether people mocked him or not. His mother was right: this was a time to stand up for Jesus.

THE FAMILY OF JESUS, *page 139*

When have you known it was time to take a stand for Jesus? How did the situation turn out?

Read Luke 24:38—49.

38"Why are you troubled?" He asked them. "And why do doubts arise in your hearts? 39Look at My hands and My feet, that it is I Myself! Touch Me and see, because a ghost does not have flesh and bones as you can see I have." 40Having said this, He showed them His hands and feet. 41But while they still were amazed and unbelieving because of their joy, He asked them, "Do you have anything here to eat?" 42So they gave Him a piece of a broiled fish, 43and He took it and ate in their presence. 44Then He told them, "These are My words that I spoke to you while I was still with you—that everything written about Me in the Law of Moses, the Prophets, and the Psalms must be fulfilled."

45Then He opened their minds to understand the Scriptures. 46He also said to them, "This is what is written: The Messiah would suffer and rise from the dead the third day, 47and repentance for forgiveness of sins would be proclaimed in His name to all the nations, beginning at Jerusalem. 48You are witnesses of these things. 49And look, I am sending you what My Father promised. As for you, stay in the city until you are empowered from on high."

What evidences for Jesus' resurrection do you see in this passage?

What did Jesus accomplish for us that we could never do for ourselves (vv. 46-47)?

What was ahead for James and other followers of Jesus (vv. 48-49)?

Never in all his life had James felt such love, sensed such grace and mercy. The nail marks were still there on His hands, but Jesus was clearly only focused on one thing.

James.

"Stay, Jesus ... Live with the family." James brought his hands together, pleading. "It can be like it was." But even as he said the words he knew the answer.

"I cannot stay." Jesus smiled, his voice warm with compassion.

James struggled to his feet and for the most wonderful moment the two of them looked at each other. Like old times. "You will always be My brother, James." Jesus stepped back. "But now you will be My disciple. And you will lead My church in Jerusalem."

"Yes, my Lord." James bowed and their eyes met once more. "I will serve You all the days of my life."

THE FAMILY OF JESUS, *pages 145-146*

LIVING IN GOD'S STORY

GOING DEEPER

Home study can help you better understand God's work in James's life—and in your own. For more insights about James in The Family of Jesus, *read chapter 5 (pp. 121-146).*

In learning to love Jesus more by studying the people who knew Him best, you can also discover principles for relating to your family. Use this unique opportunity to build a stronger home as you learn more about Jesus and His family.

DAY 1

EVERYTHING CHANGED

Read John 21:1—14.

What would it have been like for you to sit with Jesus after the resurrection? To eat with Him? To simply be together? Describe your emotions and what you might have asked Him.

How would you characterize your motivation to serve Him?

Wouldn't your motivation be so strong that you couldn't stop yourself? Wouldn't you just have to tell everyone He was alive, no matter the risk? Wouldn't you feel compelled to fall on your face to worship the living Lord? Wouldn't you be willing to do more than anything He might ask of you?

No half-hearted belief or hesitation here if you had seen the Lord, walked with Him on the Emmaus Road, or touched the nail marks of His hands. Yet, like the disciples and others who saw Him alive, we would have questions and fears, despite our joy. So much had changed.

Like James, who had known Jesus all his life, you might wish things could stay the same. Maybe like His disciples, who had walked daily with Him, you might miss the same relationship. At the same time, you knew that *everything* had changed.

What do we know about James beyond Jesus' resurrection and ascension? James and Jesus had a new and better relationship now, beyond that of family. James would express his commitment to Jesus as Savior and Lord in significant ways:

- The Book of Acts describes James as the leader of the Jerusalem church (12:17; 15:13-21; 21:18-19).

- He likely was the writer of the Book of James (Mark 6:3; Jude 1). This epistle is a series of exhortations to believers to live a consistent Christian lifestyle.

- James's ministry was to Jewish Christians who were still living by the law (Gal. 2:9). He lived scrupulously by the law so he could witness more effectively to the Jews.

- The churches he addresses by the epistle may have included congregations of Jews and Gentiles (11:20-21) and dispersed Jewish Christians.

- The term *Diaspora* refers to the scattering of the Jews beyond Palestine over several centuries. "The result of the Diaspora was that by New Testament times as many Jews lived outside of Palestine as lived within the land. In almost every city Paul visited on his missionary journeys, he found a Jewish synagogue. The Diaspora thus helped pave the way for the spread of the gospel."[10]

- James died a martyr's death approximately A.D. 60. Many believe his death was the catalyst for Vespasian's siege of Jerusalem, which caused many Christians to scatter throughout the Mediterranean region. Respect for James was so high that he was mourned by non-Christian Jews.[11]

James's guidance and exhortations continue to make a difference for Christians today who are facing the challenges of secular culture.

FAITH LIVED OUT

Read James 2:14—26.

What good is it, my brothers, if someone says he has faith but does not have works? Can his faith save him?

If a brother or sister is without clothes and lacks daily food and one of you says to them, "Go in peace, keep warm, and eat well," but you don't give them what the body needs, what good is it? In the same way faith, if it doesn't have works, is dead by itself.

But someone will say, "You have faith, and I have works." Show me your faith without works, and I will show you faith from my works. You believe that God is one; you do well. The demons also believe—and they shudder.

Foolish man! Are you willing to learn that faith without works is useless? Wasn't Abraham our father justified by works when he offered Isaac his son on the altar? You see that faith was active together with his works, and by works, faith was perfected. So the Scripture was fulfilled that says, Abraham believed God, and it was credited to him for righteousness, and he was called God's friend. You see that a man is justified by works and not by faith alone. And in the same way, wasn't Rahab the prostitute also justified by works when she received the messengers and sent them out by a different route? For just as the body without the spirit is dead, so also faith without works is dead.

What do you learn about faith and works from these verses?

FAITH	WORKS

This passage is often misunderstood and difficult to explain. The combination of challenges adds to the confusion and many false teachings about faith and works. Keep in mind a few things when you read this particular passage.

- The Book of James was written to believers. (See Jas. 1:2,16,19; 2:1,5,14; and 3:1 as a start.)

- Salvation is not due to your works. It is a gift. You are not going to lose your salvation if you fail to complete an imaginary list of good works. (See Eph. 2:8-9.)

- God has made us responsible for our actions, which have real and eternally significant results. (See 2 Cor. 3:11-15; 5:10; Rom. 14:8-12.)

Here James is referring to what others see in you. The works we do, the way we live our lives, demonstrates to others the visible evidence of our faith. Unbelievers don't see faith; they see faith lived out.

Works have no part in our salvation. Jesus Christ finished the work of salvation on the cross. We are saved only by trusting in Jesus and His finished work on the cross, not by any works or good deeds we have done.

How do you think James, the half brother of Jesus, demonstrated his faith in Jesus as the Messiah once he became a believer?

What are ways you demonstrate your faith to believers and unbelievers? How do they see a difference in your life because of Jesus?

Jesus wants you to experience the full, abundant life that comes from knowing Him and living in obedience to Him. However, many Christians serve God and their church out of a sense of obligation instead of joy.

Do you still experience the wonder and awe of your Savior? What holds you back or causes you to doubt that your faith in Him is enough? Pray and spend time thinking about the amazing gift of salvation and faith. Let Jesus remind you that He is enough.

THE POWER OF WORDS

When have you heard heart-wrenching words that hurt so much you thought you never would recover? Who spoke them, and what was the context of those words? The children's phrase "Sticks and stones may break my bones, but words will never hurt me" is used as a defense. But in real life, words do hurt.

Sometimes we are hurt most from the people closest to us. Jesus' family was no different. They loved Jesus.

Read Matthew 12:46–50.

> He was still speaking to the crowds when suddenly His mother and brothers were standing outside wanting to speak to Him. Someone told Him, "Look, Your mother and Your brothers are standing outside, wanting to speak to You."
>
> But He replied to the one who told Him, "Who is My mother and who are My brothers?" And stretching out His hand toward His disciples, He said, "Here are My mother and My brothers! For whoever does the will of My Father in heaven, that person is My brother and sister and mother."

How would you feel if a family member spoke to you this way publicly?

We are not sure exactly what James and his family felt that day, but we can sympathize with them. We, too, usually take things we hear and apply them to our feelings and self-worth. Jesus' family had something they wanted to tell Him, but Jesus was speaking to the crowds. They didn't get His attention the way they desired.

How might this scene have been different if Jesus' family had been there to listen to Him rather than to speak to Him?

When was the last time you wish you had listened instead of speaking?

Jesus made His point when He stated, "For whoever does the will of My Father in heaven, that person is My brother and sister and mother" (v. 50). Rather than rejecting His family, Jesus was actually expressing a more complete description of His mission and an expansion of the meaning of family.

Jesus' calling and purpose was to do the will of His Heavenly Father. With a few words, He spoke the truth in love to make clear to all His listeners: family are those who seek to obey God, do His will, and further His kingdom.

Read James 3:7–12.

> Every sea creature, reptile, bird, or animal is tamed and has been tamed by man, but no man can tame the tongue. It is a restless evil, full of deadly poison. We praise our Lord and Father with it, and we curse men who are made in God's likeness with it. Praising and cursing come out of the same mouth. My brothers, these things should not be this way. Does a spring pour out sweet and bitter water from the same opening? Can a fig tree produce olives, my brothers, or a grapevine produce figs? Neither can a saltwater spring yield fresh water.

What do these verses tell you about the tongue and the words we speak?

Our words often reflect the state of our heart. Over time, the truth always seems to come out.

Think of positive and negative words in your life. How have the words of others impacted you? How have words gained power over you?

Pray about the words you need to use with other people. Does some cleaning up in your heart need to take place? How will you go about making any changes necessary or allowing God to change you?

DAY 4

UPSIDE-DOWN THINKING

Have you ever spent time in a third-world country or poverty-stricken area in your own community? If so, how did that experience affect you?

Read James 2:1–7 in The Message.

My dear friends, don't let public opinion influence how you live out our glorious, Christ-originated faith. If a man enters your church wearing an expensive suit, and a street person wearing rags comes in right after him, and you say to the man in the suit, "Sit here, sir; this is the best seat in the house!" and either ignore the street person or say, "Better sit here in the back row," haven't you segregated God's children and proved that you are judges who can't be trusted?

Listen, dear friends. Isn't it clear by now that God operates quite differently? He chose the world's down-and-out as the kingdom's first citizens, with full rights and privileges. This kingdom is promised to anyone who loves God. And here you are abusing these same citizens! Isn't it the high and mighty who exploit you, who use the courts to rob you blind? Aren't they the ones who scorn the new name—"Christian"—used in your baptisms?

How does James turn upside down our assumptions about people's worth and status? How does God operate differently?

How are we to treat the world's down-and-out?

In what ways may the poor actually be rich?

Read James 2:8.

What is a practical way you can "love your neighbor as yourself" this week?

Read James 5:13–18.

In his passionate treatment of how believers should live, James talked about behaviors that did not reflect a changed heart. Even though he didn't always highlight prayer with each problem he addressed, all are helped by fervent, constant prayer.

James would encourage us to pray for wisdom, the kind that comes from above and expresses itself in humility, peace, purity, good deeds, mercy, and sincerity (see 3:13-17). To pray for help in saying the right thing at the right time and to hold our tongue on other occasions. To pray to treat all people as God's children, who have much to offer. To pray as we actively express our faith day by day.

Can you recall a time you prayed for and received what you could only describe as God's wisdom? (see Jas. 3:13-18). How did you respond?

Read James 4:7–8.

Therefore, submit to God. But resist the Devil, and he will flee from you. Draw near to God, and He will draw near to you.

WHEN TESTING COMES

For most of us, testing is a distant memory related to school days and frequent assessment. But James casts a different light on testing.

Read James 1:2–4.

> Consider it a great joy, my brothers, whenever you experience various trials, knowing that the testing of your faith produces endurance. But endurance must do its complete work, so that you may be mature and complete, lacking nothing.

According to James, what should be a Christian's attitude toward testing? What results from perseverance?

Read James 1:12.

> A man who endures trials is blessed, because when he passes the test he will receive the crown of life that God has promised to those who love Him.

What reward should we expect when we endure?

James uses the word *hypomone* to describe endurance; the meaning of the word is associated with military power and, as such, descriptive of staying power. His epistle gives us insight into the church in some of its earliest years.

What does James 1:13-15 tell us about the nature of God?

Persecution is not something we would choose for ourselves. We hurt for people who experience persecution, be it in our country or beyond. Often we hear about persecution in places we have never visited, and their policies and worldviews are very different from ours. We pray as names come to mind or as we hear mission reports.

Have you ever come close to turning away from your faith? What or who drew you back? How does that demonstrate the healing body of Christ?

James was also addressing Christians who had expected the Lord's return in their lifetime. He cautioned them not to fall into traps that would harm their witness.

Read James 5:7—11.

Who should we look to for encouragement and patience (v. 11)?

Read James 5:13—17.

What is the tool for anything we might need?

In everything pray with the active, believing faith that James admonished believers to display at all times. Pray for persevering, stand-firm faith that takes you through all kind of trials and even prepares you for persecution when it comes your way.

MARY: PRAYING AND FOLLOWING

As He came into view, Mary could see Jesus sitting on a donkey, His disciples walking beside and behind Him. All around her the people began to shout, "Hosanna to the Son of David! Blessed is He who comes in the name of the Lord!"

Mary closed her eyes and let the words of praise for Jesus wash over her soul. Yes, this was what Jesus had earned. After weeks of uneasiness and concern, after moments of all-out fear, Mary felt at peace. The people shouted the words over and over again.

Some people came running up to see what was happening. "Who is this?" they cried out.

In loud voices the crowd responded, "This is Jesus, the prophet from Nazareth in Galilee."

Like so many times in Jesus's life, Mary treasured the moment in her heart.

As Jesus reached the place where Mary stood in the crowd, He did what He often did when He was near her. He looked her way.

THE FAMILY OF JESUS, *pages 158-159*

Mary treasured Jesus and the privilege she and Joseph had been given. She loved recalling special moments as Jesus grew up. She both loved and dreaded seeing God's incarnation unfold before her very eyes, not knowing what the future would hold.

YOUR STORY

START

Everyone has a story. Enjoy sharing yours and hearing from your group as together you learn about another person in the family of Jesus—Mary.

Let's recap the family of Jesus to this point:

- Joseph—Loyal and Faithful

- Zechariah—Expectant and Trusting

- John the Baptist—Committed and Bold

- Elizabeth—Patient and Mentoring

- James—Repentant and Restored

Which family member did you relate to most when this study began? Now?

From last week, share your insights:

What are some ways people today may describe Jesus (good man, crazy, teacher, and so forth)?

When have you known it was time to take a stand for Him? What happened?

As you look ahead to Mary, consider:

What does *motherhood* mean to you?

Is there someone in your life who is always there for you, no matter the situation? How does that make you feel?

MARY'S STORY

WATCH

Watch Mary's story from The Family of Jesus Bible Study DVD *and discuss the questions with your group.*

Luke 2:25-26

Mary celebrates with other followers when Jesus did what He said He would do: when He _____ _____ _____ _____.

Luke 1:38

If He is the _____ of our story, then the story we are writing with the days of our lives will have a _____ _____ _____.

Luke 2:34-35

Promise me something: That like Mary in _____ _____ _____ _____, you will ponder in your heart what you have learned about the family of Jesus.

DISCUSS

How have you been pondering more about God's story during this study? What has He been teaching you?

What does Mary's life reveal about her?

Video downloads of this session are available for purchase at *www.lifeway.com/karenkingsbury*

If you are on social media, share what you are learning *#familyofjesus*

STUDY

MIRACLES AND THREATS

All along, Mary knew Jesus as the Messiah, seeing His life and ministry through that lens. Having known Old Testament Scriptures, she would have better understood what others could not comprehend: that Jesus was fully human and fully divine.

Read John 1:9–13.

Look for descriptions of Jesus and for how He would be received.

Four writers were inspired by the Holy Spirit to share the good news of Jesus in the Gospels; Matthew, Mark, and Luke are called Synoptic Gospels. Each had slightly different perspectives and audiences, with Mark's Gospel likely predating them.

John's Gospel introduces Jesus as God Incarnate; this Gospel is often the first Bible book a new believer reads. Matthew focuses on Jesus as the fulfillment of the Messiah prophesied in the Old Testament. Luke, a Gentile physician, includes some content not in any other Gospel, giving us unique eyewitness descriptions and teachings; he also wrote the Book of Acts, recounting the start and growth of the early church.

Mark focused on Jesus as the Son of God with authority over all humanity—including the forgiveness of sins—so miracles are prominent. The word *signs*, expressing God's miraculous activity, is prevalent in John's Gospel. A miracle can be described as something only God can do, reflecting divine intervention in human affairs.

What happened in each of these situations?

Mark 4:35-41

Mark 6:30-45,53-56

Luke 5:17-26

John 2:1-11

How does the definition of a miracle apply?

Now, more than ever, Mary was hearing of threats and plots against Jesus. The ordinary people loved Him, but the religious leaders were jealous. During worrisome and good times, Mary prayed for Jesus. But she also longed to be with Him. In reality, Mary was the only human who would be with Jesus from His birth to His death.

NO OTHER WAY?

Jesus took hold of Mary's hand. "I've been telling My disciples this. I even told them on the way into the city the other day." He paused. "Now I need to tell you."

Mary could barely breathe. If only Joseph were here to share this moment. God, give me strength ... I can't do this on my own. She struggled to speak. "Go ahead, my son."

He watched her for a while, as if waiting until He was sure she could take the impact of what He was about to say. "In the days to come I will be delivered over to the chief priests and the teachers of the law."

An ache started at the center of Mary's heart. "Jesus ..."

"There's more." He leaned closer, looking intently into her eyes. "They will condemn Me to death and hand Me over to the Gentiles to be mocked and flogged ..." Jesus hesitated. "And to be crucified."

Mary closed her eyes and shook her head. The grief coursing through her body was almost more than she could bear. This couldn't be happening. Jesus was loved by the masses. They wouldn't tolerate seeing Him crucified ... Jesus's hand was still holding tightly to her own. When she opened her eyes He was looking straight at her. "Why, Jesus?"

"These things must happen to fulfill the prophecies about Me." Peace emanated from Jesus's kind eyes. "Mother, it must be this way. I wanted you to hear it from Me."

THE FAMILY OF JESUS, *pages 163-164*

Read these Old Testament prophecies that reflect the actions Jesus knew were coming.

Betrayal—Psalm 41:9; Zechariah 11:12-13

Arrest and trials—Isaiah 53:7

Condemned to die—Psalm 22:1,7-8,18; Psalm 2:6; Zechariah 9:9; Isaiah 53:12

WITH HIM TO THE END

The same people who joyfully shouted "Hosanna," were now calling for His death.

In a place where you will not be disturbed, read Matthew 27:1-46, out loud if you like. Record your thoughts. Highlight verses in Matthew that show the ways Jesus fulfilled each of the earlier prophecies.

Betrayal

Arrest and trials

Condemned to die

Thank God for His unspeakable gift of Jesus' sacrifice to take your sin on Himself.

Read Matthew 27:45–56.

[45]From noon until three in the afternoon darkness came over the whole land. [46]About three in the afternoon Jesus cried out with a loud voice, "*Elí, Elí, lemá sabachtháni?*" that is, "My God, My God, why have You forsaken Me?" [47]When some of those standing there heard this, they said, "He's calling for Elijah!" [48]Immediately one of them ran and got a sponge, filled it with sour wine, fixed it on a reed, and offered Him a drink. [49]But the rest said, "Let's see if Elijah comes to save Him!"

[50]Jesus shouted again with a loud voice and gave up His spirit. [51]Suddenly, the curtain of the sanctuary was split in two from top to bottom; the earth quaked and the rocks were split. [52]The tombs were also opened and many bodies of the saints who had fallen asleep were raised. [53]And they came out of the tombs after His resurrection, entered the holy city, and appeared to many. [54]When the centurion and those with him, who were guarding Jesus, saw the earthquake and the things that had happened, they were terrified and said, "This man really was God's Son!"

[55]Many women who had followed Jesus from Galilee and ministered to Him were there, looking on from a distance. [56]Among them were Mary Magdalene, Mary the mother of James and Joseph, and the mother of Zebedee's sons.

What happened between noon and three in the afternoon (vv. 45-53)?

What would you have thought was happening (v. 54)? How did the centurion describe what he saw?

Read John 19:26–30.

> "When Jesus saw His mother and the disciple He loved standing there, He
> said to His mother, 'Woman, here is your son.' Then He said to the disciple,
> 'Here is your mother.' And from that hour the disciple took her into his
> home. After this, when Jesus knew that everything was now accomplished
> that the Scripture might be fulfilled, He said, "I'm thirsty!" A jar full of sour
> wine was sitting there; so they fixed a sponge full of sour wine on hyssop
> and held it up to His mouth. When Jesus had received the sour wine, He
> said, "It is finished!" Then bowing His head, He gave up His spirit."

How did Mary and Jesus show their love for each other, even at the end?

We don't know where other family members were. They may have scattered in fear;
Scripture doesn't say. We do know from these verses that Mary followed her Son to
the cross and witnessed His death, as overwhelming as that must have been. And we
know that as Her loving Son finished His work, He took care of Mary one final time.

*She found water and a cloth and gently washed the dry blood from Jesus's face and
arms. Someone brought a cloth to wrap His body, but Mary refused any help.*

*Instead she continued washing Him, cleaning Him. Her touch was gentle, the way it had
been years earlier when she had cared for the boy Jesus. Her tears helped wet His skin,
and when she had cleaned Him, she took the cloth and wrapped her son, the way she had
when He was an infant. It felt wonderful to do something, to help Him in some way. Then
Jesus's followers carried His wrapped body to the tomb. The whole time Mary stayed at
His side, right up until they placed Him in the cave. She had to be there beside Jesus.*

Her last single act of love for her oldest son.

THE FAMILY OF JESUS, *page 187*

Have you ever stayed strong for a friend or family member whose loved one was ill? You knew death was approaching, but still prayed and hoped for a different outcome.

> When the inevitable happened, how did you let go of your pent-up emotions?

> How did you grieve? Pray? Relate to other people?

You may have needed quiet and solace. The comforting presence of people for a while. Time away from some responsibilities. Restful sleep that never seemed to come. Perhaps tears fell at odd times and you had no "normal" routine.

> Why do joy and celebration often seem to occur alongside pain and sorrow? How has this been your experience?

Mary would never forget the sounds … of nails pounding into her Son's hands. Of the angry crowd. The sights … of sudden, total darkness. The smells … of blood and death. On this day, the very thought of joy seemed unthinkable.

REMEMBER AND DO NOT FEAR

Scripture doesn't tell us how Mary and her family grieved, or identify her by name as being at the tomb. Yet, it is certain Mary was devastated even as she knew God was at work. Fear was rampant and the risk of attack or arrest, possible.

There's so much we don't know but can anticipate because of what we know about Jesus' family. We know Mary's pattern of obeying God before Jesus was even born and of fully loving her eldest son, the Savior of the world, to His death.

He had tried to prepare Mary, His entire family, and His disciples. Yet no one could have imagined what happened next.

Read Matthew 27:57–66.

When it was evening, a rich man from Arimathea named Joseph came, who himself had also become a disciple of Jesus. He approached Pilate and asked for Jesus' body. Then Pilate ordered that it be released. So Joseph took the body, wrapped it in clean, fine linen, and placed it in his new tomb, which he had cut into the rock. He left after rolling a great stone against the entrance of the tomb. Mary Magdalene and the other Mary were seated there, facing the tomb.

The next day, which followed the preparation day, the chief priests and the Pharisees gathered before Pilate and said, "Sir, we remember that while this deceiver was still alive He said, 'After three days I will rise again.' Therefore give orders that the tomb be made secure until the third day. Otherwise, His disciples may come, steal Him, and tell the people, 'He has been raised from the dead.' Then the last deception will be worse than the first."

"You have a guard of soldiers," Pilate told them. "Go and make it as secure as you know how." Then they went and made the tomb secure by sealing the stone and setting the guard.

How did the officials secure Jesus' grave?

To what possibility were they responding?

Read Luke 24:1–10.

On the first day of the week, very early in the morning, they came to the tomb, bringing the spices they had prepared. They found the stone rolled away from the tomb. They went in but did not find the body of the Lord Jesus. While they were perplexed about this, suddenly two men stood by them in dazzling clothes. So the women were terrified and bowed down to the ground. "Why are you looking for the living among the dead?" asked the men. "He is not here, but He has been resurrected! Remember how He spoke to you when He was still in Galilee, saying, 'The Son of Man must be betrayed into the hands of sinful men, be crucified, and rise on the third day'?" And they remembered His words. Returning from the tomb, they reported all these things to the Eleven and to all the rest. Mary Magdalene, Joanna, Mary the mother of James, and the other women with them were telling the apostles these things.

Over the next few days Jesus appeared to all of them—even Thomas, who had doubted more than the others. More than that, He appeared to James! [see 1 Cor. 15:7]. He had said that one day His brothers would believe, and now they did. James was determined to tell everyone about Jesus. He had told her he would serve Jesus the rest of his days.

Mary had no doubt ... Jesus was alive, but something was different. And finally Mary understood. Jesus had been her son. But now He was far more: her Lord. Her risen Savior ...

Everything made sense now. Joseph's determination to rescue their son, Zechariah's song and John the Baptist's sacrifice. Elizabeth's heartache and James's epiphany. Even Mary's great anguish at the cross.

All of it had led to this. Jesus's resurrection from the dead. Indeed He had conquered death for Himself and for all people who would believe in Him. Mary lifted her eyes to heaven and took a deep breath ... Jesus's work was finished on the cross, but the cross hadn't been the end of Jesus. He would live forevermore. So that one day all those who believed in Him would also live forevermore.

THE FAMILY OF JESUS, *pages 189-190*

LIVING IN GOD'S STORY

GOING DEEPER

Home study can help you better understand God's work in Mary's life—and in your own. You may want to read the biblical narrative about Mary, in Matthew 1:18-25; Luke 1–2; John 2:1-12; 19:25-27; and Acts 1:12-14. For more insights about Mary in The Family of Jesus, *read chapter 6 (pp. 147-190).*

In learning to love Jesus more by studying the people who knew Him best, you can also discover principles for relating to your family. Use this unique opportunity to build a stronger home as you learn more about Jesus and His family.

DAY 1

WITNESS TO AN EARLY MIRACLE

Jewish weddings were community events involving extended family and friends. A festive wedding was underway in Cana of Galilee when the servants discovered something that would mar the happy day.

Read John 2:1–11.

> Who was in attendance? What happened to get Jesus involved? What was the end result?

The first of Jesus' miracles, or *signs* as the Gospel writer John communicated, resulted in Jesus' displaying His glory. It also occurred early in Jesus' earthly ministry. Importantly, His disciples "believed in Him" (v. 11). Mary was in attendance, identified though not named, and may have been helping at the wedding. Also, Jesus, His family, and His disciples (likely the five mentioned in John 1:35-51), were guests.

> How did Mary show her confidence in Jesus (see v. 5)?

Jesus' response to Mary may appear curt, but was a title of respect; He addressed Mary from the cross in the same way (see John 19:26). The answer also may have reflected His decision not to reveal Himself openly. In the Cana instance, Mary's instructions to the servants were good: "Do whatever He tells you."

Based on what you know about miracles, why would you characterize Jesus' action in verses 6-10 as a miracle?

The wedding at Cana has been described as a "quiet" miracle. A problem had come up that affected the guests' comfort and the hosts' reputation, but certainly was not life-threatening. This was not a healing or a raising-from-the-dead or a public feeding or a walking-on-water instance. Embarrassing more than anything else, the hosts had run out of wine. People would talk. Mary turned to Jesus with expectation that He could help the bride and groom avoid embarrassment.

Some think the disciples who accompanied Jesus were unexpected, adding to the head count and thus contributing to the shortage. Jesus dealt with the problem simply and quietly by instructing that water be added to the pots. They were filled to the brim and delivered to the chief servant, who tasted better wine than had been available previously. Neither the servant nor the groom knew where the finer wine had come from.

How does this miracle show God's interest in every aspect of our lives?

How do you show your confidence in Jesus, in the slightly disruptive times and in the life-changing instances?

"The number of jars (six) may indicate incompleteness since seven represented fullness." Each contained 20 to 30 gallons contributing up to 180 gallons of additional, better wine. "The Jewish purification" ritual may have involved washing of the guests' hands and certain utensils used at the wedding. Filled 'to the brim' points to the abundance of Jesus' messianic provision" (see John 3:34).[12]

PONDERING AND PRAYING

Read Luke 2:19,51.

Mary pondered Jesus' life—His birth, as well as His death—in her heart of hearts, deep in her soul. *Ponder* describes what it means to dwell on, treasure, and delight in thinking about. Mary treasured the things of God, especially her Son and Savior.

The Bible describes Mary early on as a person of reflection and prayer. Like many mothers, she began praying for her Son, the Savior, before He was born (Luke 2:19). The last mention Scripture gives of Mary, Acts 1:14, shows how she and His followers were preparing themselves for the Holy Spirit's power: "continually united in prayer."

Family members and followers of Jesus were finding prayer to be the key to a right relationship with God.

> Why do you think this is the case? How have you experienced this reality personally?

For Jesus, prayer was as natural as breathing. There was no greater joy than spending time with His Father. Every decision, big or small, was marked by prayer. Jesus' disciples could have asked Him anything and chose to ask Him to teach them how to pray. He modeled prayer with His life and with His words.

Jesus' disciples wanted to be near Him, in His presence, to know Him better. Do we have such a constant desire? We have access to the same relationship.

> How might pondering and prayer work together?

Treasuring how God had worked in the past strengthened Mary's faith for the future. Perhaps, when she didn't know how to pray, she could trust God to hear the pleading of her heart because He had heard her before. By pondering the ways He had worked in her story earlier, she could trust Him with a seemingly impossible future. Treasuring His presence helped her sense His comforting arms around her.

A timely word, perhaps through a relative like Elizabeth, could soothe her spirit and strengthen her resolve. And God certainly surprised her as He worked in amazing, totally unexpected ways.

What things of God do you ponder like Mary, expectantly looking for Him to work in your world? How does He answer you?

Do you ever pray just to seek Him, to know Him better? What are the results?

How often do you ask Him to handle something you have no idea how to handle? What are some ways He has "handled" a situation?

The best we can do for someone is to pray. Maybe the best thing we can do for our own prayer life is to ponder and treasure "all these things."

GOD'S GIFT OF GRACE

Read Romans 5:8; 6:23.

At Christmas when kids are unleashed to find their gifts under the tree, most dive in, saying, "Where's my gift? Where's my name?" They want to find their gifts! They show unbridled enthusiasm. They cannot wait to receive.

We grow up and time has its way with us. We start to hesitate. Many of us prefer to give because receiving makes us feel vulnerable. Getting indicates we are in need of something. We don't want to show that we are in need.

When the God of the universe wants to give us a gift, some of us respond by saying something like, "Oh, God, I am not worthy." The Spirit is saying back, "Of course you are not, but that was never the question anyway."

When was the last time you received a generous gift? How did you respond?

Were you embarrassed? Reluctant to accept it? At a loss for words? Wondering why someone would give so extravagantly to YOU? The next time you are given a gift, large or small, do not refuse it. Recognize it as a gift. Say thank you and accept it with humility. Acknowledge that you are someone in need of receiving a kind gesture from another—including from God.

List some of the many gifts God has given you and thank Him for them. Ask Him to help you know who needs the gift of friendship (or other gift) from you, and commit to follow up this week.

THE ONLY WAY?

In "Mary: The Loving Mother," I wrote about a touching time Jesus might have had with Mary before His arrest and crucifixion, to prepare her for what was to come. So she could pray in the knowledge that God's plan was being fulfilled. This encounter is tender, potentially representing the last time Mary saw Jesus before His arrest and crucifixion. When they were about to part, He reminded her:

> *"I want you to remember this moment. Remember I told you these things would happen ... They have to take place. It's God's will, Mother." He took both her hands. "Okay?"*
>
> THE FAMILY OF JESUS, *page 166*

And her reply in this scenario was a question. *There's no other way?* Many today still ask, *Was there no other way?* We cringe at the thought of such a brutal death. What did it accomplish? Crucifixion was ghastly, hard to comprehend then and now. Still other people are of the opinion that there are many ways to God. To have only one way available to us goes against our human nature.

Read Romans 5:12.

What problem does our nature create?

Read Romans 5:6—11.

Who was able to satisfy our sin problem? How?

Read 1 Corinthians 15:1—14.

Why is the resurrection so essential to salvation?

Without the resurrection, sin and death would still win. Instead, Christ has overcome so that we might be in right relationship with God and live with Him eternally.

Jesus is the Source of eternal life and wants to be the doorway to new life for you. John 1:29 and other instances describe Jesus as called the "Lamb of God." In the Old Testament, sacrifices were made for the sins of the people, and Jesus became the sacrificial lamb for your sin. Jesus is the New Covenant between God and humanity.

During His earthly ministry Jesus said, "I am the way, the truth, and the life. No one comes to the Father except through Me" (John 14:6). He is waiting for you now.

Admit to God that you are a sinner. Repent, turning away from your sin.

Read Romans 3:23; 6:23.

Believe in Jesus Christ as God's Son and receive Jesus' gift of forgiveness from sin. He took the penalty for your sin by dying on the cross.

Read John 3:16.

Confess your faith in Jesus Christ as Savior and Lord.

If you confess with your mouth, "Jesus is Lord," and believe in your heart that God raised Him from the dead, you will be saved. One believes with the heart, resulting in righteousness, and one confesses with the mouth, resulting in salvation (Rom. 10:9-10).

If you are not a believer, you can accept His invitation and receive Jesus Christ into your life today. Share your decision with another person, perhaps your pastor or a Christian friend. Following Christ's example, ask for baptism by immersion in your local church as a public expression of your faith.

If you are a Christian, celebrate again the joy of your salvation. Reflect on the people and circumstances leading up to your salvation experience. How did you realize you were a sinner? Who cared enough to share Jesus with you? How has your life changed since that day?

HOW DO WE REMEMBER?

Memories. They are a beautiful and precious treasure. There are so many things we forget in life, but other memories we ponder and recall until the day we die.

> What are some of your most precious memories? Think about the sights, sounds, smells, and feelings of those memories. How does the memory bring your senses alive again even after 10, 20, 40, or even 60 years?

Many people in the Bible took time to remember. They remembered who God was and what He had done. His promises. His faithfulness. They remembered.

Moses is just one example of a person who came to the end of his life and remembered. In Deuteronomy 32 the Israelites were encouraged to "remember the days of old" and their past (v. 7). After remembering some of both the good and the bad, Moses blessed the twelve tribes of Israel. He gave them hope for their future and something precious to remember and hang on to.

> What do the following examples of remembrance encourage you to recall, or how do they give you hope?
>
> Psalm 103:2
>
>
> Matthew 26:26-28
>
>
> John 14:26
>
>
> Romans 5:8

Romans 10:9

Philippians 1:1-6

2 Timothy 3:16

1 Peter 5:7

Just as we remember so many things about our family members, so did Jesus' family remember Him.

If you were to guess, what do you think each of the people we have studied in Jesus' family most remembered about Jesus?

Joseph, His earthly father

Zechariah, His uncle

Elizabeth, His aunt

John the Baptist, His cousin

James, His half brother

What do you suppose were Jesus' thoughts and feelings toward His family?

And finally, think about Mary. We have the benefit of holy Scripture to know and recall how God has worked throughout His story. For many, like Mary, treasuring the memories was the main way to recall God's work. What we treasure in our hearts is the direction and focus our lives will take.

If Mary were to write in her journal about Jesus, what would she say? What would she pray? What was it like to be the mother of Jesus? What would she remember most about Him? What moments and memories were most precious to her? Many times in Jesus' life, Mary would treasure a special moment in her heart.

As Jesus reached the place where Mary stood in the crowd, He did what He often did when He was near her. He looked her way.

THE FAMILY OF JESUS, *page 159*

May you always remember and treasure the tender moments when Jesus looked your way and you sensed His Spirit moving in your life and in your heart. Remember that, like the family of Jesus, you are not forgotten. He has plans and purpose for your life. He looks your way.

THE Family of Jesus

APPENDICES

These articles provide additional background on topics of interest. They are not required to teach or participate in the Bible study. In addition, articles from *Biblical Illustrator* magazine are available online (*www.lifeway.com/karenkingsbury*) to enhance your understanding of the people and times in *The Family of Jesus Bible Study*.

Visions, Dreams, and Angels in the Bible

God used visions in the Old Testament to reveal His plan, carry out His plan, and put His people in places of influence. For example, God restated His covenant with Abraham through a vision (Gen. 15) and, using Joseph as interpreter, explained the meaning of Pharaoh's dreams to him (Gen. 41). It was in a dream that Solomon asked for, and was granted, wisdom (1 Kings 3). There are a number of instances in both the Old and New Testaments of activity by angels.

According to Scripture, angels are messengers of God, created beings (Col. 1:15-16), usually invisible (Ps. 148:2,5; Col. 1:16), with the capacity to take on different forms (Ex. 3:2). While angels as a whole are not winged beings, there are some biblical references to angelic creatures as "winged" or "flying" (Ex. 25:20; Isa. 6:2; Rev. 14:6). They are personal beings with will and intelligence, though finite (2 Sam. 14:20; Rev. 22:6). They are restricted to accomplish only what God allows (Ps. 103:20). Angels often display emotions, such as joy over repentance (Luke 15:10; Matt. 18:10) and compassion (Luke 16:22).

In the Bible, angels fulfill these purposes:

- To praise and glorify God (Luke 2:13-14)
- To minister to and protect believers (Acts 5:19-20; 12:7-11; 27:20-25; Luke 16:22)
- To strengthen Jesus and to defend Him (Mark 1:13; Luke 22:43; Matt. 26:53)
- To reveal and communicate God's message to humans (Luke 1:13-20,26-39; Acts 8:26; 10:3-4; 11:13; 12:7-11)
- To administer judgment, at God's call, on His enemies (2 Kings 19:35; Acts 12:23; Rev. 16)
- To accompany the Lord when He returns (Matt. 25:31)

After careful consideration about Mary's pregnancy, Joseph would have divorced (Matt. 1:19-20). Comforted and assured by the angel that Mary's pregnancy was of God, Joseph went ahead with the marriage. Later, after Jesus was born, God sent two more dreams, "one to tell Joseph to take his family to Egypt so Herod could not kill Jesus and another to tell him Herod was dead and that he could return home" (see Matt. 2:13,19-20).[1]

God primarily uses the Bible to communicate with people today, though He can and will communicate any way He chooses. In unreached areas or mission fields, people often recount having a dream of someone coming to tell them about Jesus. It is always wise to compare any revelation to God's truths as expressed in the Bible.

Marriage and Divorce in Bible Times

Betrothal was a legal process reflecting the couple's commitment to each other in advance of a formal wedding ceremony. Jewish marriage had a degree of formality with certain prescribed steps.

The father of the groom initiated plans for a wife for his son. "Many young girls were promised at birth by their fathers and as they grew older, were only passive participants in the transaction. The more legal 'betrothal' usually took place when the daughter became of marriageable age and about one year prior to the wedding ceremony." The Jewish father of the bride drew up a contract, called the *ketuba*, which was witnessed by both families. Gifts were exchanged, including a dowry (*mohar*) to seal the covenant between the two families.[2] The betrothal period lasted a year during which time the couple lived apart and solemnly prepared for marriage.

Jewish girls often wed between age 13 and 16 while it was common for young men to marry between 18 and 20. Mary likely was young, due to the fact that Mark 6:3 identifies a number of siblings in Jesus' family—"James, Joses, Judas, and Simon? And aren't His sisters here with us?"

Often unmarried daughters tended their father's flock (Ex. 2:16), worked in the field, or otherwise rendered help. Upon her marriage, a young woman would be thought of as increasing the efficiency of her husband's family and diminishing that of her parents. Therefore, the young man must offer adequate compensation—thus, the marriage dowry.[3]

A promise of marriage was different from betrothal; it could be set aside. Betrothal was more binding than contemporary engagement. God's blessing was asked on the solemn commitment being made by these two people. In the eyes of the law, their status was the same as being married but without coming together as one.

Mary became pregnant during the betrothal period so the divorce Joseph considered (Matt. 1:19) would be required for the two to sever their commitment. "Joseph seemingly considered his predicament in light of Old Testament Scriptures. For example, Deuteronomy 2:20-21 suggests stoning women who were guilty of adultery. Another choice allowed the man to write a 'divorce certificate' if he found his wife to be 'displeasing.' "[4]

The wedding ceremony itself was festive, often lasting up to seven days with music, dance, and food. It celebrated the couple's monogamous relationship for life. Prior to the wedding ceremony, the bride underwent ritual cleansing and adornment for the groom. Friends and family accompanied her from her father's house to the groom's house, or their home together.

For the wedding ceremony itself, often at night, only a few were invited. Blessings were pronounced on the couple and a marriage contract read. In the privacy of the bridal chamber (*huppa*) the bride and groom consummated the marriage. Many people were invited to the marriage feast that followed.

For centuries it was possible for a husband in Arab lands to divorce his wife by a spoken word. The Mosaic Law limited the power of the husband to divorce his wife, by requiring he give her a written bill of divorcement (Deut. 24:1). The sin of adultery did not have anything to do with divorce under Jewish law. That sin was punishable by death (Lev. 20:10; Deut. 22:22), and that by stoning.

If a husband found any unseemly thing in his wife, he could give her a written bill of divorcement and send her away, which made it possible for her to marry another man (Deut. 24:2). A man guilty of unfaithfulness was considered to be a criminal only in that he had invaded the rights of another man.

"By the first century, in Rome and Greece a marriage could be terminated by the woman or man. However, the Jewish law remained in force that divorce was the right of the husband only."[5]

What Happened During Those 400 Years?

Silence spanning four centuries is unique to human history. That is how long it had been since the nation of Judah—God's chosen people—had heard from Him. Not since the time of the prophet Malachi had Judah heard the voice of God. What was happening as the Israelites waited?

Three major time periods comprise what is called the Intertestamental Period: Greek (323-167 B.C.); Jewish independence (167-63 B.C.), and Roman (63 B.C.—A.D. 70). Shortly before 600 B.C. the Babylonians had captured Jerusalem, taking many of the people away as captives. After Cyrus overcame the Babylonians, the Jews who so desired could return. The Temple was rebuilt. During the times of Nehemiah and Ezra, the Jewish religious community established itself, and the worship and life of the people continued.

Greek Period—In a series of battles, Alexander gained control of territory from Asia Minor to Egypt, including Palestine and the Jewish people. In 331 B.C. Alexander gained full control of the Persian Empire. He is credited with several contributions, including introducing Greek culture and ideas, establishing cities and colonies in the conquered territory, and spreading Greek language throughout the region.

After Alexander's death, his generals established control over different parts of the empire. Ptolemy and Antigonus struggled for control of Palestine, which continued to be a point of contention between the Ptolemies and Seleucids. The Jews generally fared well under the Ptolemies, with self rule and a continuation of religious practices.

Antiochus III (the Great) attempted to take Palestine from the Ptolemies in 217 B.C. without success. However, in 198 B.C., he defeated Ptolemy IV, and he and his successors ruled Palestine until 167 B.C. The situation of the Jews changed after Antiochus was defeated by the Romans in the battle of Magnesia (190 B.C.). The burden of the Jews increased.

When Antiochus IV Epiphanes sought to acquire Egypt, the Romans confronted him and he backed off, returning to Jerusalem. He found the city in full revolt. He allowed his troops to kill many Jews and determined to put an end to the Jewish religion.

Jewish Independence—When officers attempted to compel leading citizens to offer sacrifices to Zeus, conflict broke out. Jewish leadership fell to Judas, nicknamed Maccabeus the Hammerer because of his success in battle. His men were devoted to obedience to the law and worship of God. Regaining control of the Temple around

164 B.C., he had it cleansed and rededicated. This action is still commemorated in the feast of Hanukkah.

Hyrcanus, who became high priest and civil ruler (134-104 B.C.), destroyed the temple of the Samaritans on Mt. Gerizim. He conquered the ancient kingdom of Edom, forcing people to emigrate or convert to Judaism. It is from this people that Herod the Great would come.

Approximately 67 B.C. civil war broke out, lasting until 63 B.C. Aristobulus was driven back to Jerusalem, where he encountered Roman resistance and, later, Pompey. Aristobulus tried to fight the Romans, but was defeated and taken prisoner. The Romans had taken control of Palestine.

Roman Period—Under the Romans, the Jews paid heavy taxes but did not experience changes in religious practices. Antipater was named governor of Palestine; Hyrcanus, high priest. The situation was unstable.

Herod, a son of Antipater's, was made king in 40 B.C., at the urging of Antony and Octavian. King until 4 B.C., Herod's rule was a time of turmoil for the Jewish people. He had been forced to convert to Judaism but people never accepted him; he represented a foreign power. He later proved to be an efficient administrator for Rome, keeping the peace among people who were hard to rule.[6]

This eventful yet lengthy period of silence was about to change.

Zechariah and Elizabeth seemingly were the perfect couple, with both being from priestly families: he from the division of Abijah, and she from the daughters of Aaron. Yet all was not perfect; for years they longed for a child but had not had one. The social stigma of barrenness often left couples bitter, as they were considered unworthy to possibly be the parents of the Messiah. Yet, Zechariah and Elizabeth remained faithful, trusting that God would fulfill His will for their lives and somehow, some way, sometime provide that missing piece to their otherwise perfect lives.

Zechariah served in the temple two weeks a year. His duties varied depending on three things: the number of priests on hand, the activities scheduled for the week, and the casting of lots. The priests cast lots to discern whom God had chosen to perform the duties of highest honor.

One duty was to offer incense. Because the number of priests was so large, this duty was assigned only once in a priest's lifetime. In Exodus 30:7-8, God had commanded Aaron to burn incense on the golden altar in the tabernacle both in the morning and evening so there might be a perpetual sweet aroma to the Lord.

The Scriptures associate burning incense with prayer (Ps. 141:2; Rev. 5:8; 8:3). As the aroma of the incense rises into the nostrils of God, so do prayers rise to His ears. The tradition of using incense continued into the New Testament era. For Zechariah to offer the incense, then, was the summit of his priestly ministry.

That the pinnacle of his priestly ministry occurred at the exact time of God's renewed communication with His people is no coincidence. Elizabeth's barrenness was by God's design and was ultimately to be for God's glory. Her son was destined to be the forerunner of the Messiah, thus the timing of his birth had to be in harmony with the timing of the Messiah's advent. Elizabeth's barrenness and the Lord's 400-year silence were broken simultaneously in one event: God's announcing the coming of the forerunner of the Messiah.[7]

During the reign of Herod, Jesus was born. He was the king who ordered the execution of the male babies in Bethlehem. At his death, Herod willed his kingdom to three of his sons: Antipas, tetrarch of Galilee and Perea; Philip, tetrarch of Gentile regions northeast of the Sea of Galilee; and Archelaus, king of Judea and Samaria. Archelaus, deposed in A.D. 6, proved to be a poor ruler. His territories were placed under direct rule of Roman procurators under the control of the governor of Syria.[8]

What the Cross Accomplished

To understand what Jesus accomplished on the cross is to understand the gospel. To believe personally that what Christ did on the cross He did for you, is to believe the gospel of Jesus Christ.

Christ's death on the cross must be understood in two broad ways: First, when Jesus was nailed to the cross, the Father charged to Him all of our sin (2 Cor. 5:21) and judged the full penalty of our sin on Jesus as He died (Col. 2:14).

Second, Jesus conquered the power of Satan, darkness, and death as He died for our sin (Col. 2:15; Heb. 2:14), thus establishing His supreme authority and power over everything in creation (Eph. 1:20-23). To summarize, in His death on the cross Jesus paid the penalty for our sin, and He totally defeated the power of sin.

Jesus' subsequent resurrection from the dead was not just a nice ending to the story but rather necessary evidence that His death for sin really worked (1 Cor. 15:17). The penalty of sin is death and the greatest power that sin has over us is death. But since the penalty of sin is death, and since Christ paid the penalty of sin fully by His death on the cross, His resurrection from the dead demonstrated that the penalty had been paid in full … His resurrection also demonstrated that the complete power of sin had been defeated as He arose victorious from the grave …

If we will trust fully Christ's accomplishment for us—that He paid sin's penalty and conquered sin's power—and not look to our own works or accomplishments as if they could commend us to God, we will be saved (Eph. 2:8-9).[9]

Continue in Bible Study

Perhaps you are new to Bible study and have questions about the best way to learn more. Hopefully, you have fallen in love with Scripture during this study and want to dive in deeper.

Similar Bible studies keep you connected to believers who are learning from God's Word, too. They provide you a specific time and place to focus on some aspect of the Bible and its application to life. However, nothing compares to a daily personal encounter with God. Here are some reasons and benefits. We study the Bible to:

- Know the truth. We want to think clearly about what God says is true and valuable (see 2 Pet. 1:20-21).

- Know God in a personal relationship (see 1 Cor. 1:21; Gal. 4:8-9; 1 Tim. 4:16).

- Live well for God in this world. Living out His will expresses our love for Him (see John 14:23-24; Rom. 12:2; 1 Thess. 4:1-8; 2 Tim. 3:16-17).

- Experience God's freedom, grace, peace, hope, and joy (see Ps. 119:111; John 8:32; Rom. 15:4; 2 Pet. 1:2).

- Grow spiritually as we reject conformity to the world and are changed by the renewing of our minds (see Rom. 12:2; 1 Pet. 2:1-2).

- Minister to other Christ followers and to those who have yet to respond to the gospel (see Josh. 1:8; 2 Tim. 2:15; 3:16-17; Eph. 6:11-17; 2 Pet. 2:1-2).

- Guard ourselves from sin and error (see Eph. 6:11-17; 2 Pet. 2:1-2).

- Build up as a Christian community with others in the body of Christ (see Acts 20:32; Eph. 4:14-16).[10]

If you do not already have a daily quiet time, commit to selecting a special time and place. Choose the time of day that works best for you, and make it a priority. Keep your Bible and study materials in your meeting place. Develop a balanced plan for Bible reading, such as *A Reader's Guide to the Bible*. Make notes to see how God is speaking, and respond to Him in prayer. Strive for consistency as your main goal.[11]

Start a Toolbox

As you can, begin to build a Bible study toolbox of resources to enhance your understanding of the Bible. A good study Bible in an understandable translation is essential. In choosing a Bible translation, look for one that uses the earliest and most reliable Hebrew and Greek manuscripts. Some translations seek to approximate word-for-word correspondence with the Hebrew or Greek text while others seek to capture the sense of the author's intended meaning in highly readable language.[12] Other helpful tools are a concordance and Bible dictionary.

Here are features of each Bible study tool to enhance your study:

Bible atlas—Maps, charts, and photographs that illustrate the land, sites, and archaeology of the ancient world of the Bible

Bible dictionary—Alphabetical list of key terms, places, people, events, and concepts in the Bible

Bible encyclopedia—Articles about Bible characters, events, and places, including history, religious environment, culture, language, and literature, as well as cross-references to related Scripture verses

Bible handbook—Brief commentary, maps, historical background, archaeological background, kings, genealogies, and other information about the Bible.

Bible commentary—Detailed theological analysis of specific verses and passages of Scripture. Includes a background introductory section for each book of the Bible, followed by detailed commentary of Scripture verse by verse

Bible concordance—Alphabetical index of important words in Scripture and the references of texts in which they are found

Topical Bible—Bible references to topics addressed or mentioned in the Bible

Online resources—The website *www.mystudybible.com* offers free online tools for reading and studying the Bible.[13]

Begin to Memorize Scripture

As you develop in your understanding of the meaning of Scripture, consider committing verses to memory. You will be surprised how often a word from God comes to mind at just the right time. Here are some steps to get started:

1. *Begin with a positive attitude.*—Many people think they cannot memorize, but you can do all things through Christ (Phil. 4:13).

2. *Glue the reference to the first words.*—To remember both the verse and the references, say the reference and the first words without pausing. For example, "Philippians 4:13—I can do all things."

3. *Memorize bite by bite.*—Memorizing a verse phrase by phrase is easy because you are only learning five or six words at a time.

4. *Review, review, review.*—Consider using memory cards to review. After memorizing the verse, review every day for 90 days, weekly for the next six weeks, and monthly for the rest of your life.

5. *Meditate on the verse.*—Meditation can increase your grasp of the passage's teaching and application.

6. *Use spare time wisely.*—Use your mobile devices or carry Scripture-memory cards to use during your spare time or when exercising or waiting in line.

7. *Team with a friend.*—Listen to each other's verse, checking the Bible or card for accuracy.[14]

Endnotes

Sessions

1. "Messiah," *Holman Illustrated Bible Dictionary* (Nashville: Holman Reference, 2003), 1111.

2. 2 Samuel 7:4-17, *Matthew Henry's Concise Commentary on the Bible*. Volume 6. As quoted on Bible Gateway. [online] [cited 22 April 2014]. Available from the Internet: *www.biblegateway.com*.

3. Tony Evans, *The Power of God's Names Bible Study* (Nashville: LifeWay Press, 2014), 154.

4. Ibid., 155.

5. Ibid.

6. *Holman Christian Standard Study Bible,* Matthew 3.

7. Charles A. Ray, "John the Baptist: His Life and Ministry," *Biblical Illustrator,* Fall 2007 (Nashville: LifeWay, 2007), 78.

8. "Mentor," *Merriam-Webster's Unabridged Dictionary*. [online] [cited 15 April 2014]. Available from the Internet: *www.merriam-webster.com*.

9. Rhonda Kelley, *Life Lessons from Women in the Bible* (Nashville: LifeWay Press, 1998), 90.

10. "Diaspora," *Holman Illustrated Bible Dictionary*, 421.

11. Eusebius, *Ecclesiastical History, Loeb Classical Library, Books 1-V,* trans. Kirsopp Lake (Cambridge: Harvard University Press, 1992, II, xxiii in John Polhill, *Biblical Illustrator,* Spring 2005), 78-81.

12. *Holman Christian Standard Study Bible,* John 2.

Appendices

1. "How did God use dreams and visions in the Bible?" Joseph. Got Questions Ministries © 2002-2013. [online] [cited 25 April 2014]. Available from the Internet: *www.gotquestions.org*.

2. Mona Stewart, "First-Century Marriage Customs in Israel," *Biblical Illustrator,* Winter 1999-2000, 22-24.

3. "Manners & Customs: Marriage Customs" Bible History Online, Vancouver, W.A. [online] [cited 25 April 2014]. Available from the Internet: *www.bible-history.com*.

4. Roberta Jones, "Of Marrying Age," *Biblical Illustrator,* Winter 2011-12,16.

5. Stewart, 24.

6. "Intertestamental History and Literature," *Holman Illustrated Bible Dictionary* (Nashville: Holman Reference, 2003), 829-833.

7. James Wiles, "Zechariah and Elizabeth: A Silence Broken," *Biblical Illustrator,* Winter 2007-08, 26.

8. Ibid., *Holman Illustrated Bible Dictionary*, 833.

9. Excerpted from Bruce A. Ware, "The Cross and the Gospel," *HCSB Study Bible* (Nashville: B&H Publishing Group, 2010), 1846-47.

10. George H. Guthrie, *Read the Bible for Life* (Nashville: LifeWay Press, 2010), 16.

11. Ibid., 18.

12. Ibid., 23.

13. Adapted from *Read the Bible for Life Leader Kit*. Item 005253507. Published by LifeWay Press®. © 2010 George H. Guthrie. Made in the USA. Reproduction rights granted.

14. Thomas D. Lea, *God's Transforming Word: How to Study Your Bible* (Nashville: LifeWay Press, 1986), 12-13. Out of print.

LEADER GUIDE

Your commitment to facilitate *The Family of Jesus Bible Study* will impact you as well as the women in your group. God desires to challenge, strengthen, and solidify your walk with Christ as you pray, prepare, and guide this study. These suggestions are for six 60- to 90-minute group sessions. Adapt to the needs of your group.

- Reserve your meeting space and secure a DVD player and television. If possible, position the furniture so everyone can see both the DVD and one another. The room builds expectations and helps direct the group's focus.

- Enlist volunteers to help with promotion, snacks, childcare, or other needs.

- Read *The Family of Jesus* hardback book that is in the Leader Kit. You can read the stories about each character prior to that week of study or in whatever time frame works best. As you read, note page numbers or segments that make an impact. Consider developing additional questions to promote discussion and application. Or use questions or statements in emails to encourage women during the week.

- Be prepared to facilitate more than lecture. When you ask a question, allow participants time to think and process before answering. However, when needed, clarify, expand, or rephrase a question. Assess thoughts and opinions by asking a "What are your thoughts about …" type of question. Your goal is to promote conversation and involvement. Let everyone know her thoughts are valued and that you desire interaction and full participation.

- As facilitator, you have authority to rein in tangents and bring the discussion back on topic. Also, feel free to adjust the leader guide to accommodate and provide the best experience for your group. Don't feel obligated to get through everything. Often the best questions lead to intense conversations and deeper study into the Scripture. At the same time, respect women and their time.

- If your time is limited to 60 minutes, try to do the video and selected pages in the Study section. Encourage women to continue their study at home.

- This Bible study has strong potential for outreach through a neighborhood/ home study or a book club. Consider strategic locations and women who might facilitate as hostesses as well as facilitators.

- Consider different ways to involve the women in your group. Note how some exercise leadership and involve them in leading small-group activities.

- *The Family of Jesus Bible Study* leader kit includes a video message to leaders, a segment to promote this study, and Karen's testimony.

Session 1
Joseph: Husband, Protector, Servant

In Advance
Read Joseph's story from *The Family of Jesus* hardback book and mark pages to share with the group. Preview DVD Session 1 and page 13 in *The Family of Jesus Bible Study*.

START 10-15 MINUTES

Welcome participants. Distribute name tags, asking women to write their names and the name of a favorite person in the Bible. Briefly introduce yourself and share one of your favorite Bible characters. Depending on the size of the group, ask women to share their names and choices.

Briefly introduce the study, including Karen Kingsbury, the format of the Bible study, and each week's group time. Encourage women to find time to complete the home-work between group sessions to get the most out of the Bible study.

Lead women through "Your Story" (p. 12), explaining how each week's group time begins with this segment. Ask women to form smaller groups of five or fewer.

WATCH AND DISCUSS 30-35 MINUTES

Direct women to the viewer guide on page 13. Play the DVD (27:50) and share using the "Discuss" questions.

STUDY JOSEPH'S STORY 15-30 MINUTES

Read aloud the excerpt at the top of page 14. Remind women that everywhere they see such a shaded area with the title *The Family of Jesus* and a page number, they are reading from Karen Kingsbury's book. She helps bring alive the people in Jesus' family so we can understand them better and realize that they were real people.

Lead the group through as much as possible of pages 14-17. Read Scripture passages aloud and discuss questions as time allows. (If your time is short, focus only on pp. 16-17.) Conclude by asking women to share something new or fresh about Joseph.

Ask women to turn to page 18 in their member books. Encourage them to complete "Living in God's Story" before the next group meeting. Challenge them to note new truths they learn or are reminded of as they complete the homework, plus any questions for next week.

Follow up by emailing or calling all participants, thanking them for their participation. Share new insights from Joseph's story. Let women know that you are praying for them as they dive deeper into their study of Joseph this week.

Answer key to prophecy exercise, page 19:

OLD TESTAMENT PROPHECY   NEW TESTAMENT FULFILLMENT

Jesus would be:

Born of a woman (Genesis 3:15)   Matthew 1:22-23; Luke 1:26-31

Born in Bethlehem (Micah 5:2)   Matthew 2:1; Luke 2:4-6

Born of a virgin (Isaiah 7:14)   Luke 1:32-33; Romans 1:3

Descended from Abraham   Matthew 1:20; Galatians 4:4
(Genesis 12:3; 22:18)

Heir to King David's throne   Matthew 1:1; Romans 9:5;
(2 Samuel 7:12-13; Isaiah 9:7)   Galatians 3:8,16

Session 2

Zechariah: Singing A New Song

In Advance

Read Zechariah's story from *The Family of Jesus* hardback book. Mark any specific pages that would be good to read aloud or discuss with the group. Preview DVD Session 2 and page 35 in *The Family of Jesus Bible Study*.

START 15-20 MINUTES

Welcome women back and introduce newcomers. Distribute name tags and invite participants to share challenges and rewards of their first week of study. Share your comments about finding a time and place daily to complete homework. Ask women for any tips they have discovered that make study time more productive.

Review by asking volunteers to share answers to these questions from homework on Joseph; if you have less time or prefer, use review questions on each week's Start page beginning with this session:

- What relationship did Jesus come to establish?

- What expectations do you have of the Son of God?

- How do you explain the "coincidences" of your life? What do you attribute only to God?

- How would you describe your thoughts and emotions when you find yourself in a waiting period and all you hear is silence?

Remind women that "Your Story" is a way to review and connect the previous session with the next family member of Jesus. Ask participants to turn to page 34 in their member books and lead them through "Your Story."

WATCH AND DISCUSS 30-35 MINUTES

Direct women to the viewer guide (p. 35), play the DVD (27:02), and debrief the video using the "Discuss" questions.

STUDY ZECHARIAH'S STORY 15-30 MINUTES

Read aloud the "Waiting and Watching" section on page 36. Then ask women to form four groups of two to three people each (if a larger group, form groups of three to four each and assign the same passages several times). Assign each group one of the Scriptures from pages 36-39: *Luke 1:5-6; Isaiah 40:3-5; Luke 1:13-17; Luke 3:2-6; Luke 1:67-79*. After 10 minutes, ask each group to share one thing they discovered.

Distribute blank notecards and invite women to share a prayer request, her name, and how you might pray for her during the week. Close in prayer. Follow up by emailing each woman and sharing a Scripture that might apply to her request.

Answer key to similarities/differences between angelic announcement to Zechariah and to Mary, page 36: angels announced both births; both births were unusual, involving the Holy Spirit; both sons fulfilled Old Testament prophecies.

Session 3
John the Baptist: Completing God's Task

In Advance
Read John the Baptist's story from *The Family of Jesus* hardback book. Mark any specific pages that would be good to read aloud or discuss with the group. Preview DVD Session 3, along with page 55 in *The Family of Jesus Bible Study*.

START 15-20 MINUTES

Welcome women and ask them to share in pairs something they learned about Joseph or Zechariah in the previous two weeks of study. Ask how this week's study on Zechariah encouraged, frustrated, or challenged them.

Briefly review. Call for several volunteers to share responses to any of these review questions from the homework about Zechariah.

- Like Zechariah, how can you cultivate a song of joy that overflows and sustains you?

- How will you continue to have hope when it seems your prayers go unanswered?

- How is bringing up the next generation to know God part of your intentional parenting?

Ask participants to turn to page 54 in their member books to continue their review of Zechariah and make the connection with John the Baptist. Lead the group through "Your Story."

WATCH AND DISCUSS 30-35 MINUTES

Direct women to the session's viewer guide (p. 55) and play the DVD (29:47). Use the "Discuss" questions to get women's insights.

STUDY JOHN THE BAPTIST'S STORY 15-30 MINUTES

Lead the group through "Legacy and Purpose" (p. 56). Encourage those who do not have a legacy of faith to be the starting point for faith foundations for their families. Ask volunteers to read *Jeremiah 1:5; Mark 10:44-45;* and *Ephesians 1:18.* Discuss the question, What perspectives about calling do these verses provide?

If time allows, instruct women to complete pages 58-61 in groups of three or four. Or challenge them to add it to their homework for the week.

Encourage women to be diligent in their study this week. Remind them to pray for one another and for the legacy of faith they are creating for their families. Close in prayer, asking God to help the women to discover a new hunger for God's Word.

Session 4
Elizabeth: Holding Out Hope

In Advance

Read Elizabeth's story from *The Family of Jesus* hardback book. Mark any specific pages that would be good to read aloud or discuss with the group. Preview DVD Session 4 along with page 77 in *The Family of Jesus Bible Study*.

START 15-20 MINUTES

Welcome women back to the small group. Encourage them to mingle.

Call for responses to several review questions from the John the Baptist homework:

- Do you find that your to-do list never ends? Is there any margin for error if your schedule is delayed? What are some tasks or responsibilities for which it is time to say no?

- What are some examples of times when you gave up doing something good so that you could pursue what was best? How difficult was it to say no to some things in order to say yes to others?

- When Jesus has taken hold of your life, how do you live? How do you make the most of your time for His kingdom, for His plans, and for His purposes?

Remind women that each week starts with review and connecting. Ask participants to turn to page 76 in their member books, and lead them through "Your Story."

WATCH AND DISCUSS 30-35 MINUTES

Direct women to the session viewer guide (p. 77) and play the DVD (27:10). Use the "Discuss" questions to further build a connection with Elizabeth.

STUDY ELIZABETH'S STORY 15-30 MINUTES

If your time is short, focus on pages 78-79 and complete the reading and search of Scripture. If time allows, work through all of pages 78-83 as a large group or in small groups.

Make assignments to women in order to complete these pages. Ask one woman to serve as a *narrator*, reading information that ties the passages together. Assign the second woman to *read all the shaded sections* from *The Family of Jesus* book. Ask the third woman to read all the *questions* and the fourth, the *Scripture passages*.

- What do you learn as you connect Zechariah, John the Baptist, and Elizabeth together as a family and as part of the greater family of Jesus?

Close in prayer for yourself and each woman in the group. Ask them to help you reach out to anyone who started the study but has been absent.

Session 5

James: From Skepticism to Commitment

In Advance

Read James's story from *The Family of Jesus* hardback book. Mark any specific pages that would be good to read aloud or discuss. Preview DVD Session 5, along with page 97 in *The Family of Jesus Bible Study*.

START 15-20 MINUTES

Greet each woman by name as she arrives. Begin with prayer before reviewing.

Call for responses to selected review questions from the homework on Elizabeth.

- What burden did Hannah carry (1 Sam. 1:5-7)? What did she do about it (1:10-11)? What happened, according to verses 19-20? What similarities do you see in John the Baptist's birth (see Luke 1:5-25,57-66; also refer to 1 Sam. 2:1-11)?

- How did God answer both Abraham and Elizabeth, according to His timing and plan?

Ask participants to turn to page 96 in their member books. Lead the group through "Your Story."

WATCH AND DISCUSS 30-35 MINUTES

Direct women to the session viewer guide (p. 97). Play the DVD (30:03) and use the "Discuss" question to draw out insights.

STUDY JAMES'S STORY 15-30 MINUTES

Create groups to complete the different sections on pages 98-103 ("Crazy Big Brother?," "A Different Messiah," and "Taking A Stand"). Ask groups to search the Scripture references, answer the questions, and prepare to present their findings to the group. Discuss one question from each section of study:

- What are some descriptions people today give of Jesus?

- In what ways do you think Jesus' own family might have felt rejected by Jesus?

- When have you known it was time to take a stand for Jesus?

Remind women that the next session is the last. Encourage women to finish their homework and to take time to review the past weeks' studies. Close in prayer. Follow up with an email affirming how you have seen God at work in each woman's life during this study.

Session 6
Mary: Praying and Following

In Advance

Read Mary's story from *The Family of Jesus* hardback book. Mark any specific pages that would be good to read aloud or discuss with the group. Preview DVD Session 6 along with page 117 in *The Family of Jesus Bible Study*.

START 15-20 MINUTES

Welcome women back. Open with prayer, thanking God for each woman, the study, the lessons learned, and for His faithfulness as we all journey with Him.

Review the James homework by asking women to respond to any of these questions.

- How do you think James, the half brother of Jesus, demonstrated his faith in Jesus as the Messiah once he became a believer?

- How are we to treat the world's down-and-out?

- What is the tool for anything we might need?

Ask participants to turn to page 116 in their member books, and lead the group through "Your Story."

WATCH AND DISCUSS 30-35 MINUTES

Direct women to the viewer guide on page 117. Play the DVD (31:15) and use the "Discuss" questions to debrief.

STUDY MARY'S STORY 15-30 MINUTES

Read aloud "No Other Way?" from page 119. Then read John 19:26-30 and the rest of page 122 with the group. Discuss how group members think the family of Jesus felt when they finally reached this point in His life.

Close by reading Luke 24:1-10 and the highlighted story on page 125.

- How does hearing Mary's story and the truth of Scripture encourage you?

- How does the resurrection of Jesus give you hope as you walk through this life?

- Review what you hoped to get out of this study. How has learning about the family of Jesus changed you?

Content in day 4, "The Only Way?," concludes with a plan of salvation (pp. 131-132). Point out this information and be sensitive to the Holy Spirit's convicting work in your group.

Encourage women to complete the homework for Mary's story and to consider how her life fits into God's greater story this week. Point out that day 5, pages 133-35, will help them remember the study and the truths they've learned.

Close with a time of prayer. Be available after the session to talk more with women.

Optional Session 7

If women would like to meet for an additional group time, here are some follow-up questions from day 5 to use for discussion:

If you were to guess, what do you think each of the people we have studied in Jesus' family most remembered about Jesus?

Joseph, His earthly father
Zechariah, His uncle
John the Baptist, His cousin
Elizabeth, His aunt
James, His half brother
Mary, His mother

What do you suppose were Jesus' thoughts and feelings toward His family?

FROM #1 *NEW YORK TIMES* BESTSELLING AUTHOR

KAREN KINGSBURY

COMES A FRESH LOOK
AT THOSE CLOSEST TO JESUS

THE
Family of
Jesus

BOOK ONE

THE COMPLETE STORIES OF

Joseph, Zechariah, John the Baptist,
Elizabeth, James, and Mary

AVAILABLE WHEREVER
BOOKS ARE SOLD OR AT
SIMONANDSCHUSTER.COM

HOWARD
BOOKS

LIFE-
CHANGING
BIBLE
STUDY
SERIES

LET'S BE
FRIENDS!

VISIT OUR LIFEWAY WOMEN'S BLOG AT
lifeway.com/allaccess

LifeWay | Women